Ancient Israel

HARRY M. ORLINSKY

Hebrew Union College—Jewish Institute of Religion
New York

*

Cornell University Press

ITHACA, NEW YORK

THE DEVELOPMENT OF WESTERN CIVILIZATION

*Narrative Essays in the History of Our Tradition from
Its Origins in Ancient Israel and Greece to the Present*

EDITED BY EDWARD W. FOX

Ancient Israel

BY HARRY M. ORLINSKY

Foreword

THE proposition that each generation must rewrite history is more widely quoted than practiced. In the field of college texts on western civilization, the conventional accounts have been revised, and sources and supplementary materials have been developed; but it is too long a time since the basic narrative has been rewritten to meet the rapidly changing needs of new college generations. In the mid-twentieth century such an account must be brief, well written, and based on unquestioned scholarship and must assume almost no previous historical knowledge on the part of the reader. It must provide a coherent analysis of the development of western civilization and its basic values. It must, in short, constitute a systematic introduction to the collective memory of that tradition which we are being asked to defend. This series of narrative essays has been undertaken in an effort to provide such a text for the introductory history survey course offered in the College of Arts and Sciences of Cornell University. It is being published in the present form in the belief that the requirements of this one course reflect a need that is coming to be widely recognized.

Now that the classic languages, the Bible, the great historical novels, even most non-American history, have dropped out of the normal college preparatory program, it is impera-

tive that a text in the history of European civilization be fully
self-explanatory. This means not only that it must begin at
the beginning, with the origins of our civilization in ancient
Israel and Greece, but that it must introduce every name or
event that takes an integral place in the account and ruth-
lessly delete all others no matter how firmly imbedded in
historical protocol. Only thus simplified and complete will
the narrative present a sufficiently clear outline of those
major trends and developments that have led from the beginning of our recorded time to the most pressing of our
current problems. This simplification, however, need not in-
volve intellectual dilution or evasion. On the contrary, it can
effectively raise rather than lower the level of presentation.
It is on this assumption that the present series has been based,
and each contributor has been urged to write for a mature
and literate audience. It is hoped, therefore, that the essays
may also prove profitable and rewarding to readers outside
the college classroom.

The plan of the first part of the series is to sketch, in related essays, the narrative of our history from its origins to
the eve of the French Revolution; each is to be written by a
recognized scholar and is designed to serve as the basic reading for one week in a semester course. The developments of
the nineteenth and twentieth centuries will be covered in a
succeeding series which will provide the same quantity of
reading material for each week of the second semester. This
scale of presentation has been adopted in the conviction that
any understanding of the central problem of the preservation of the integrity and dignity of the individual human being depends first on an examination of the origins of our
tradition in the politics and philosophy of the ancient Greeks
and the religion of the ancient Hebrews and then on a rela-

tively more detailed knowledge of its recent development within our industrial urban society.

The decision to devote equal space to twenty-five centuries and to a century and a half was based on analogy with the human memory. Those events most remote tend to be remembered in least detail but often with a sense of clarity and perspective that is absent in more recent and more crowded recollections. If the roots of our tradition must be identified, their relation to the present must be carefully developed. The nearer the narrative approaches contemporary times, the more difficult and complicated this becomes. Recent experience must be worked over more carefully and in more detail if it is to contribute effectively to an understanding of the contemporary world.

It may be objected that the series attempts too much. The attempt is being made, however, on the assumption that any historical development should be susceptible of meaningful treatment on any scale and in the realization that a very large proportion of today's college students do not have more time to invest in this part of their education. The practical alternative appears to lie between some attempt to create a new brief account of the history of our tradition and the abandonment of any serious effort to communicate the essence of that tradition to all but a handful of our students. It is the conviction of everyone contributing to this series that the second alternative must not be accepted by default.

In a series covering such a vast sweep of time, few scholars would find themselves thoroughly at home in the fields covered by more than one or two of the essays. This means, in practice, that almost every essay should be written by a different author. In spite of apparent drawbacks, this procedure promises real advantages. Each contributor will be in a position to set higher standards of accuracy and insight in an essay encompassing a major portion of the field of his life's work than could ordinarily be expected in surveys of some ten or twenty centuries. The inevitable discontinuity of style and interpretation could be modified by editorial co-ordination; but it was felt that some discontinuity was in itself desirable. No illusion is more easily acquired by the student in an elementary course, or is more prejudicial to the efficacy of such a course, than that a single smoothly articulated text represents the very substance of history itself. If the shift from author to author, week by week, raises difficulties for the beginning student, they are difficulties that will not so much impede his progress as contribute to his growth.

This essay, *Ancient Israel,* by Mr. Harry M. Orlinsky, is written to provide a brief narrative account of the history of the peoples who created the Hebrew Bible and, at the same time, to outline the integral relationship between the development of their society and the growth of the Biblical tradition. The importance of this subject can hardly be overstated. Not only do we draw our earliest and deepest social and moral—not to mention religious—concepts from the experiences of ancient Israel, but throughout its entire history western European civilization has maintained the Bible as the central document of its cultural inheritance. Therefore, any heir of the western European tradition who would understand the development of his society must at once look for its earliest roots in Biblical society and study not only the content, but the expression, of its principal moral precepts in the Biblical writings. It is hoped that this essay will provide an introduction to both aspects of the subject and, while indicating the significance of the historical origins of our tradition, will lead the reader to return to a new reading and new understanding of the Bible itself.

Any study of the Bible presents great difficulties. Not only do religious convictions and emotions permeate the field, making any clear summary extremely difficult, but in recent years the complexity of the subject has been vastly increased by startling archaeological discoveries in Israel and the Near East. So far this wealth of new materials has not been fully assimilated. Altogether, the difficulties confronting the author have convinced the editor of the need for far more extensive scholarly apparatus than would normally be appropriate to an essay of this type. Some footnotes have been included primarily for the use of more advanced readers and the bibliography has been divided into two sections, one intended as suggestions for the general reader and the second for the benefit of students of the Bible.

Needless to say, the organization of such a vast range of new materials within such a difficult field has called for frequent consultation with other scholars in the field. Both author and editor wish to express their gratitude to Dr. Solomon Grayzel, Dr. Benjamin Maisler (Mazar), Dr. Ellis Rivkin, Dr. G. Ernest Wright, and Dr. Kenneth E. Stein. Miss Linda Altman, with the aid of Dr. Israel Renov, is responsible for the maps.

Edward Whiting Fox

Ithaca, New York
January, 1954

Contents

Maps

Introduction

THE tribes of Israel, though small in numbers and relatively late to arrive, were destined to remain unique among the many peoples who appeared in western Asia at the dawn of history. Out of their way of life grew three great religions, the Jewish, the Christian, and the Moslem.

The history and religious experiences of the Israelites are interwoven in a collection of writings called the Bible. No other single book, or collection of books, has played so important and prolonged a role in the development of western civilization.[1] Indeed, the simple use of the word Bible, which derives from Greek *ta biblia* "the books," with no more identification than the capital "B," points to its significance as "the Book" *par excellence.*

Influence of the Bible

No other description is needed because the Bible has constituted the supreme religious and moral fount and authority

---

[1] Cf. the opening statement in P. Marion Simms, *The Bible in America: Versions That Have Played Their Part in the Making of the Republic* (New York, 1936), Introduction, p. 1: "The Bible as a book stands alone. The vast majority of all the books that have ever been published has been Bibles."

for the numerous nations who have professed the Hebrew, Christian, and Moslem faiths. The moral codes of western Europe have drawn heavily on the ethical teachings of the Bible, particularly on the concepts of social justice which the prophets so forthrightly and dramatically expressed. Indeed, it is generally accepted that the spirit and the democratic ideals of the Constitution of the United States derive in some measure from this Biblical inheritance.

As literature, too, and as a factor in the development of the literature of western culture, the Bible has no equal. There is scarcely a book in the Bible which has not been described at some time as a literary masterpiece. The Book of Job was described by Carlyle as "the grandest book ever written with pen." The Book of Ruth has frequently been cited as a model of short-story writing. Such books as Psalms and the Song of Songs have probably never been matched. If, as has been said, great literature is the expression of arresting thoughts in brilliant diction, then the poetry of Amos, Isaiah, Jeremiah, and other prophets are supreme examples of their kind.

In the matter of influence, it is generally recognized that English literature cannot be understood apart from the Bible. In its classical English form, the King James Version, the Bible has constituted from the beginning a standard of prose style. No other single work, be it Latin, Greek, or English, has so deeply affected the style and thinking of English writers.

What Is the Bible?

The Bible is a collection of various kinds of writings composed in different periods which came in time to be regarded as divinely inspired sacred scripture. These writings deal with the career of Israel from its beginning shortly after the twentieth century B.C. until the successful Maccabean war of independence of the Jews against Hellenistic Syria in 165 B.C. To the Jews, the Bible consists of twenty-four books.[2] During the first four centuries A.D. the Christian Church compiled an additional twenty-seven books, and named them the New Testament, to distinguish them from the Old Testament, the term which it came to use for the Hebrew Bible. In addition, the Roman Catholic Church recognized several other books, which it introduced into the Old Testament. The Protestant Church, however, followed the Jewish tradition in rejecting these additional books, which are now generally known as the Apocrypha.[3] For the purposes of this essay the Bible will be accepted to mean the twenty-four books of the Hebrew Bible.

The Threefold Division of the Bible

The first, and most authoritative, division of the Hebrew Bible is the Law, or the Five Books of Moses, sometimes called the Pentateuch. These five books include Genesis, Exodus, Leviticus, Numbers, and Deuteronomy. This section contains two kinds of material: historical and legal, both terms being taken in their widest sense. The historical data relate the story of mankind, as understood by the

[2] The Hebrew Bible is sometimes said to consist of thirty-nine books. This number is reached by reckoning as separate books each of the two parts of Samuel, Kings, and Chronicles, each of the twelve so-called minor prophets (see below), and Ezra and Nehemiah. See, e.g., S. B. Freehof, *Preface to Scripture* (Cincinnati, 1950), pt. II.

[3] See C. C. Torrey, *The Apocryphal Literature* (New Haven, 1945); R. H. Pfeiffer, *History of New Testament Times, with an Introduction to the Apocrypha* (New York, 1949); S. Zeitlin and S. Tedesche, *The First Book of Maccabees* (New York, 1950), in the Dropsie College edition of *Jewish Apocryphal Literature.*

Biblical writers, from the Creation until the days of Abraham (Genesis 1-11), proceeding from there to the career of the Hebrews in Canaan, Egypt, and the wilderness of Sinai, up to the death of Moses on the eve of the invasion of Canaan in the thirteenth century B.C. The legal part details the essential constitution of Israel.

The second great division of the Bible, the Prophets, consists of eight books and covers a period lasting about 750 years. In this epoch, Canaan was conquered, Israel's united and divided kingdoms rose and fell, and the state of Judah and the Temple of Solomon were restored, in part, after the Babylonian Exile, at the end of the sixth century B.C.

During this phase, the role of the prophetic movement was dominant. First of all, its adherents took the royal archives and other source material and wove them together carefully and vividly into a social and political history of Israel, carving out for themselves, in the process, a reputation as the world's first systematic historians. The books of Joshua, Judges, I and II Samuel, and I and II Kings—these books are sometimes called the Former Prophets—constitute this great achievement. Secondly, in intervening in the political and social life of their fellow Israelites, the prophets expressed their ideas so forthrightly and in such beautiful and powerful poetry that they placed themselves forever among the greatest social moralists of all time. The books of Isaiah, Jeremiah, Ezekiel (the so-called Major Prophets) and the twelve so-called Minor Prophets—among whom Hosea, Amos, and Micah stand out—are the repository of this unsurpassed material.

The third and final division of the Bible is called the Writings, or the Hagiographa. This section consists of eleven books which run a considerable gamut in variety of style and content, and nearly every one of which is a classic in its own right. Devotional literature is well represented by the familiar Book of Psalms. Wisdom literature, the speculation of what constitutes the good life and the practical means of achieving it, is exhibited in such books as Proverbs, Job, and Ecclesiastes. The Song of Songs is a lyrical poem of love, tender and passionate; in later times the lover and his beloved became identified with God and His beloved people Israel. The Book of Daniel, in its final form a product of the second century B.C., tells a dramatic story of the purported career of a Judean youth living in the Babylonian Exile in the days of Nebuchadnezzar (early sixth century B.C.), a time which to this day symbolizes for the Jews the pit of despair. Daniel's dreams and visions, which among other things supposedly foretell Maccabean victory over Syria about 165 B.C., became the forerunner and model of the apocalypses or supernatural revelations which appeared first in Jewish and then in Christian literature.[4] The memoirs of Ezra and Nehemiah constitute both interesting autobiography and important source material for the restoration of Judea after the Babylonian Exile. These postexilic memoirs appear to have been edited by the person who wrote the Book of Chronicles, which provides a survey of Biblical history from Adam to Nehemiah (about 400 B.C.). Chronicles is the last of the twenty-four books of the Hebrew Bible.

The Bible as History

The Bible is the major source for our knowledge of the history of Israel in ancient times; yet its value for

[4] See Joshua Bloch, *On the Apocalyptic in Judaism* (Philadelphia, 1952), in the *Jewish Quarterly Review Monograph Series*, No. 2.

the historian has not always been appreciated sufficiently.

Until the eighteenth century the Bible was universally accepted as a trustworthy history book of antiquity. Indeed, the Book was regarded as being literally true, the Creation, the Flood, Noah's Ark, the walls of Jericho, and all. But as the Age of Reason dawned and in turn gave way to nineteenth-century philosophies of evolution and scientific materialism, the Bible, in common with the New Testament and all records of antiquity, Greek, Roman, and the rest, came to be very considerably discounted as a reliable basis for the reconstruction of history.

The heroic doings of the patriarchs, Abraham, Isaac, and Jacob, as described in the Book of Genesis, were discounted as mere myth. The very existence of Moses was doubted. Joshua was believed to have had little or nothing to do with the Israelite conquest of Canaan. David and Solomon were considered greatly overrated. Extensive parts of the prophetic books were attributed not to the prophets themselves but to redactors and disciples who lived several centuries later in different circumstances. The story of the Babylonian Exile was relegated to the realm of fiction. And so on.

This negative attitude to the Bible was reflected in more recent times, for example, in the writings of the well-known social philosopher Bertrand Russell, and the historiographer R. G. Collingwood. In his popular *History of Western Philosophy* [5] Lord Russell wrote:

The early history of the Israelites cannot be confirmed from any source outside the Old Testament, and it is impossible to know at what point it ceases to be purely legendary. David and Solomon may be accepted as kings who probably had a real existence, but at the earliest point at which we come to some-

[5] New York, 1944.

thing certainly historical there are already two kingdoms of Israel and Judah [ninth century B.C.].

And a year later, in his posthumous book on *The Idea of History*,[6] Collingwood dismissed in less than one page as "theocratic history and myth" the entire Biblical material.

It is unfortunate that these scholars—and there are very many more—have not kept up with the more recent discoveries and analyses of the ancient Near East. For today, in considerable degree, the pendulum has swung the other way. Modern historians do not, to be sure, accept every part of the Bible equally as literal fact. Yet they have come to accept much of the Biblical data as constituting unusually reliable historical documents of antiquity, documents which take on new meaning and pertinence when they are analyzed in the light of the newly discovered extra-Biblical sources. Indeed, even the mythical parts of the Bible are now generally regarded as reliable reflection of fact, empirically grounded, and logical in their way. It is a question of understanding the perspective and circumstances involved.

Archaeology and the Bible

This radical re-evaluation of the significance of the Bible has been necessitated by the archaeological discoveries of the past three decades. The civilizations which flourished in the Fertile Crescent of old are better known today than anyone before World War I thought possible. The material, social, and religious configurations of the Sumerian, Egyptian, Babylonian, Hurrian, Assyrian, Canaanite, Hittite, and Aramean societies can be delineated to an increasingly satisfactory degree. It is now possible to see the entire

[6] Oxford, 1945.

ancient Near East from a thoroughly new perspective, and so it has become necessary to re-examine the Biblical record in the light of our broadened understanding. More and more the older view that the Biblical data were suspect and even likely to be false, unless corroborated by extra-Biblical facts, is giving way to one which holds that, by and large, the Biblical accounts are more likely to be true than false, unless clear-cut evidence from sources outside the Bible demonstrate the reverse.

The Bible as Sacred History and Its Interpretation

From the foregoing it would seem that it is possible, at long last, to write a thoroughly acceptable history of ancient Israel, one which will conform to the highest standards of modern, scientific historiography; yet the fact is that the time has not yet come, and well may never come, for such a work to be achieved. The major problems that confront the modern historian in handling the sources of the Biblical period are twofold. First, the historian cannot fulfill his task when his sources are inadequate and of uncertain authorship and date. The sources for Biblical history are even now neither sufficient nor chronologically secure. It is only occasionally that a Biblical book, or its component parts, can be ascribed to a definite time, place, author and purpose; and, furthermore, extensive as the extra-Biblical material has become, it generally suffices only for the broadest sort of understanding. Secondly, in the handling of the Biblical material there is the major problem of discovering the fundamental economic, social, and political forces from documents couched almost exclusively in religious terminology and given to interpret all historical experiences as manifestations of divine intervention.

Those who were responsible for the composition of the Hebrew Bible believed that what they uttered and wrote derived from the God who had entered into a mutual Covenant with Israel. According to the terms of the Covenant, God loved and protected Israel and no other people, and Israel worshiped no other god but Him. The modern historian, however, cannot accept such an interpretation, but must seek—behind the religious terminology—the same kind of documented human story, with an examination of its underlying dynamics, that would be his proper objective in any other field. Otherwise he would achieve no more than a compilation of myths, chronicles, annals, oracles, autobiographies, court histories, personal apologia.

The historian cannot regard any human activity or statement, be it religious or secular, sacred or profane, as beyond his domain. His competence is limited only by the nature and adequacy of his sources. The limitations inherent in the Biblical sources thus militate against an historical reconstruction which will be clear in every respect; in spite of these inherent difficulties, scholarly researches have been supplying flashes of light where none existed before. So the work of interpretation goes on, some results of which form the basis of this essay.

The Fertile Crescent: Hebrew Origins

THE Near East, that quadrangle of land lying between the Mediterranean, the Caspian and Red Seas, and the Persian Gulf, and connecting Asia with Africa, is in general a barren and uninviting area. Running across it, however, from the alluvial flatlands of the Tigris and Euphrates in the southeast through Syria in the northwest, and then curving down along the coast of Palestine to the Nile Delta, lies a crescent-shaped region of rich, well-watered land (see Map I). It was in this Fertile Crescent that the first great civilizations appeared and that man first made the transition from hunting, fishing, and cave dwelling to systematic farming within an organized community of his fellow kind. From this focus, the new mode of civilization extended to lower Mesopotamia, and from there to the Syro-Palestinian coast, to Egypt, to the Anatolian plateau, to the Indus Valley in Pakistan, to Crete, and to Greece. The caves of Mount Carmel in modern Israel have provided the best materials for identifying the stage at which food-gathering man began systematically to abandon the cave to establish food-producing villages.

I. The ancient Near East in the patriarchal period (second millennium B.C.).

The Ancient Near East

This change began during the latter stages of the Neolithic or Late Stone Age, about 6000–4500 B.C. In ever-increasing numbers people learned to cultivate cereal grasses and prepare more grain than was immediately needed. Once there were food surpluses, latent human energies were released. The arts of animal husbandry, of making wattle huts from mud smeared on sticks—these and other advances occurred in this period. The first crude villages appeared, sometimes, as at Jericho, in association with a shrine.

A series of metallurgical discoveries accelerated this process of social organization. During the Chalcolithic, or Copper-Stone Age, about 4500–3000 B.C., man learned how to smelt copper for use in tools, weapons, and ornaments, and gradually this malleable, if none-too-plentiful, substance superseded stone. Silver and lead came into use in several parts of the Near East, and tin bronze had been discovered, though it was only rarely used, before 3000 B.C. Other technical advances followed. The wheel and the plough were invented, and a rudimentary division of labor was introduced. Houses made of mud brick replaced mud-walled huts, and in the manufacture of the bricks themselves fine stone aggregate eventually replaced chopped straw. Houses came to have wooden roofs, and even smoothly plastered walls sometimes decorated with geometric patterns in several colors.

During the Early Bronze Age, about 3000–2000 B.C., the general population increased, and large groups of people shifted about. Sumer, Akkad, Egypt, and other dynastic civilizations emerged. In this period, villages grew into cities, canals were dug to irrigate the land, architecture became monumental, men labored in organized groups. The early

Egyptian dynasts built pyramid tombs, and the rulers of Mesopotamia erected structures in the form of tiered brick mounds, the ziggurats. Pictographic and cuneiform writing were invented, enabling the priestly and ruling classes to keep records and other professional data, such as magical spells. Henceforth, too, knowledge could be stored for the use of posterity. These early civilizations bred others as they interpenetrated and competed. Mesopotamian influences became apparent in Egypt, by way of Syria and Palestine; and Egypt, in turn, began to extend political dominion to Palestine and Syria.[1]

Growth of Cities

By this time man had become in every sense a thinking, planning, and articulate human being, with a clear idea of hierarchy in respect of class and occupation. As we have noted, villages which once had consisted of patriarchal family groups coalesced into cities, and these cities merged into "city-states," that is, urban centers controlling satellite territory. The family commune was replaced by a governing assembly of adult freemen, this assembly usually headed by a council of elders. Women, children, slaves, and the unpropertied were excluded from the assemblies. Slavery had become an economic institution, the earliest known instance of human chattels. These earliest slaves were foreign captives of war.

As the population increased, the elders began to assume the right, particularly in times of crisis, of electing a king, while retaining at all times the legal right to depose him. But

[1] Cf. V. Gordon Childe, *New Light on the Most Ancient East* (New York, 1953); R. J. Braidwood, *The Near East and the Foundations for Civilization* (Eugene, Oregon, 1952).

with still further increase in the size and complexity of human settlements, kings became a permanent feature of the prevailing social order. The idea of a dynasty, or kingly line, followed in due course. Fixed rules for adjudicating anarchic private differences appeared, and legal codes began to be compiled, of which two dating from about 1950 B.C., over two centuries before the great code of Hammurabi, or Hammurapi, have now been excavated.

Mythology, Religion, and Science

When not warring, building, tilling the soil, and tending his flocks, man began to inquire about the nature of the universe and his place in it. Literary masterpieces were created in Sumerian, Akkadian (the cuneiform Semitic language of the Babylonians and Assyrians), and Egyptian. They represented an effort to determine the origin and to evaluate the activity of the sun, the moon, the planets, the other heavenly bodies; of the rain, wind, storm, and similar phenomena; of farming and shepherding; of human life and death, of the relationships among men, of the career of man on earth and thereafter; of justice, of good and evil, of reward and punishment. In brief, as today, so then too, man attempted to learn who really ruled the universe, and how to get the most out of it for himself during his relatively brief stay in this world.

In this early period, the existence of the gods in the upper and nether worlds and their intervention in human affairs on the earth played a dominant role in the thinking of the people. They knew little or nothing of the why and how of natural phenomena. The all-important cycle of the growth, death, and rebirth of vegetation upon which their agricultural economy depended was attributed to supernatural powers of different gradations, to higher gods and lower gods. Men explained the origin of the gods and of their functions to the best of their rather meager knowledge in the light of their geographical environment and social experience.

Mythology and religion came to be important factors in the personal and social life of men, and myths, like religions, were seized upon by those in power, as well as by those who sought to attain power, in their own interests. Kings, priests, government and military officials, landowners, merchants— all strove to make the religious and mythological thinking of the people serve their own ends. Eventually, a self-perpetuating priestly class took shape, an intelligentsia which devoted all its time to exploring and exploiting divinity. Pantheons of gods, with appropriate mythologies and rituals of appeasement and propitiation, crystallized out of the primitive animism of prehistory, or that kind of subreligion in which all natural forces and objects are indiscriminately endowed with demonic power. Deity, like humanity, became organized.

An agricultural society needed a way of measuring time, in order to prepare for flood, drought, heat, cold, and other seasonal fluctuations. The obvious clock was the sun, moon, and the conspicuous stars, which never vary, as shepherds since time immemorial must have observed during the watches of the night. The empirical data derived from the observation of the heavenly bodies were utilized for omens. Star watching as a regular occupation naturally fell to the priests, the superior ones who could read, write, and use numbers. Thus astronomy was incorporated into the religious apparatus, and acquired ceremonial significance, both in Egypt and Mesopotamia. A knowledge of time measurement also sharpened the chronological, or historical, sense.[2]

Empires and Nomads

Western Asia was being constantly overrun and criss-crossed by many vigorous unsettled groups of people from 2200 to 1800 B.C. The Fertile Crescent, producing as it did surplus wealth, frequently attracted the more primitive peoples living in the grasslands and in the highlands. The archaeological work accomplished recently in this area has produced a generally clear picture of the situation. The first identifiable people to settle permanently in Mesopotamia were the Sumerians, about 3000 B.C. In the earlier part of the third millennium, many Sumerian city-states were overrun by groups of Semites, and about 2300 B.C. the first empire in history was established by King Sargon of Akkad. About a century later a number of groups of people north and east of Akkad formed a coalition, and destroyed this Semitic empire. From about 2070 until 1960 B.C. the Sumerians succeeded in recapturing a goodly portion of their former glory, only to disappear forever as a sovereign people before the onslaughts of several peoples from different directions. Chief among these were the Semitic Amorites from western Asia and the Elamites from the region southeast of Mesopotamia. The Amorites proceeded increasingly to dominate much of western Asia, including Syria and Palestine, and reached the peak of their influence first in Mari on the Middle Euphrates (near the modern Iraq-Syria border) and then in Babylon in the days of Hammurabi (about 1728–1686).

Another important ethnic element in the Fertile Crescent in the first half of the second millennium was the Hurrians

[2] See Otto Neugebauer, *The Exact Sciences in Antiquity* (Princeton, 1952), pp. 91 ff.

(Biblical Horites). Shortly before 2000 B.C. they began to come down in ever-increasing numbers from the mountainous regions northeast of Mesopotamia, and by the end of the fifteenth century they were to be found in every part of western Asia, including Syria and Palestine, in many instances alongside the Amorites. The Hurrians attained their greatest prominence in the Mitanni Kingdom (about 1470–1350 B.C.), which extended from the region east of the upper part of the Tigris to the Mediterranean coast of Syria.

Hebrew Beginnings and the Habiru

In this period and area of ethnic movements, the group from which the Hebrews of the Bible finally emerged took its place in documented history. From about the twentieth century B.C. to the twelfth a group of people appear in Near Eastern documents. They are called Habiru or Hapiru, and with them are associated the names SA.GAZ and Apiru; neither the original forms of the names nor their meanings have yet been determined. These documents derive from Mesopotamia, Asia Minor, Syria, Palestine, and Egypt.

To the limited extent that these sporadic and incomplete data permit one to draw some conclusions, it would seem that at about 2000 B.C. there arose a term Habiru as a name for various unsettled groups of people, Semitic and non-Semitic, chiefly the former. They wandered about as semi-nomads from one area to another, sometimes with their own flocks and sometimes as skilled craftsmen, as smiths, musicians, and the like. At other times they made sudden raids on caravans and on weak, outlying communities, or else hired themselves out for specific functions and periods of time, for example, as mercenaries and as private or government slaves. Not infrequently they became prisoners of war and state slaves doing forced labor (*corvée*). In several instances, individual Habiru rose to prominent status—for example, in the land of the Hurrians in northern Mesopotamia (about 1400 B.C.), in Assyria (about 1150), and in Babylonia (about 1050). Some of the Habiru settled down in conquered towns and regions and ceased to wander.

There appears to be good reason for associating the Biblical Hebrews with some of these far-flung Habiru. The Biblical account places the career of the Hebrews within the general orbit of the activities of some of the Habiru groups in the different lands of the Near East and in the different epochs of the second millennium B.C.; this can scarcely be merely a series of many remarkable coincidences.

Hebrew origins begin essentially with Abraham the son of Terah (Genesis 11), whose origin is located in the region of Ur in southern Mesopotamia, less than thirty miles from Larsa, where Habiru are found about 1900 B.C. Ur was an extremely important center in this very period. Terah is said to have moved with his household about six hundred miles to Haran in northwestern Mesopotamia, and after Terah died Abraham took his own immediate family and began the long journey to Canaan. Abraham retained contact with his family in Haran, to the point of seeking out a wife for his son Isaac from the family of Laban, grandson of Abraham's brother Nahor. Isaac's son Jacob also went to this region to acquire a wife, of the family of the same Laban. Haran was a flourishing city in the Balikh Valley at this time, and Habiru were found there in this period.

Habiru dwelt in the northwest part of the Babylonian empire during the eighteenth and seventeenth centuries B.C., the period made famous by King Hammurabi, and in the succeeding centuries they inhabited many of the Hurrian-controlled parts of western Asia. The Book of Genesis especially, dealing with the ideas and customs of the patriarchal period of the Hebrews, reflects clearly this early milieu of the Babylonians, Amorites (western Semites), and Hurrians. The prophet Ezekiel, in the sixth century B.C., knew well this fact when he addressed Jerusalem in the following words: "Your origin and your birth are of the land of the Canaanite; the Amorite was your father, and a Hittite was your mother" (16:3, 45).[3] It is now known that when Rachel took the "teraphim" (household objects, perhaps gods) of her father Laban (Genesis 31), it was probably to give her husband Jacob some kind of authority; among the Hurrians the possession of the household gods gave their owner property rights.

Many of the Biblical personal names in the patriarchal period are typical of the names employed in western Asia, especially among the Amorites, in the first half of the second millennium. Among these names may be cited Terah, Serug his grandfather, Nahor his father and his son, Haran and perhaps Abraham (or Abram), his other sons, as well as Jacob and Benjamin.

The Biblical writers recognized many groups of Hebrews in different times and lands, just as the contemporaneous, extra-Biblical records indicate the existence of many groups of Habiru throughout the Fertile Crescent during the second millennium B.C. When Terah left Ur for Haran, he left behind him the Hebrew family of his married son Nahor, from

---

[3] All English translations of the Hebrew text of the Bible cited in this essay are the author's own; he consulted occasionally the *Jewish Publication Society Translation* (Philadelphia, 1917) and the *Revised Standard Version* (New York, 1952). Chapter and verse numbers refer both to the Hebrew Bible and to the King James Version and the Revised Standard Version, unless otherwise indicated.

whom ultimately there came such peoples as the Arameans
(Genesis 11:26 ff.; 22:20–24). In fact, Nahor's son Bethuel,
Abraham's nephew, is referred to in the Bible (Genesis
25:20) as an Aramean; and Abraham's grandson Jacob, who
married Bethuel's granddaughters, Leah and Rachel, is described once as "a nomad (or, wandering) Aramean"
(Deuteronomy 26:5). In Canaan, Abraham's nephew Lot
raised a considerable Hebrew family, from which there developed, among others, the two kindred nations of the
Hebrews, the Moabites and the Ammonites (Genesis 19).
Abraham's son Ishmael (since Mohammed, the traditional
ancestor of the Arabs), born to him by Hagar the Egyptian
maidservant of Sarah, gave rise to a large and varied number
of tribes (Genesis 25:12–18); and the same is true of the
progeny born to Abraham by his second wife, Keturah—
notably, the Midianites (25:1–4). Isaac's older son Esau was
the progenitor of a very abundant and important number of
tribes and peoples, including the Amalekites and the Edomites (Genesis 36).

There is considerable similarity between the Hebrews and
a number of the non-Hebrew descendants of Abraham in
the kinds of personal names employed by them. Such names
as Bela, Saul, and Achbor are Edomite as well as Hebrew
(Israelite). Jobab is an Arabian, an Edomite, and also an
Israelite name. Reuel is the name borne by a son of Esau (by
his wife Bosnath, a daughter of Ishmael), by Moses' Midianite father-in-law, and by a member of the tribe of Gad; in
abbreviated form, Reu, it is the name also of Abraham's
great-grandfather. But this point need not be labored here
further.

It is an interesting fact that the term Habiru ceased to oc-
cur in extra-Biblical sources at about the same time that the

term Hebrew ceased to be used in the Bible. Before the end of the second millennium, those of the Habiru groups which had conquered and become associated with specific territories acquired new, national names; the rest of the Habiru had become absorbed by the various settled communities in which they found themselves. The story of the name "Hebrews" is about the same. Originally associated with some of these far-flung Habiru groups, the Hebrews of the Bible came in time to lead a career of their own in a specific region, namely, Canaan; and the name Hebrews gave way to the name Israelites (literally, "Children of Israel") when the nation came into being. The other Habiru groups which had become nations in their own right acquired new names too: Moabites, Ammonites, Edomites, and Midianites. Thus the Biblical term Hebrew was never employed for the nation any more than the term Habiru was.

A notable similarity between the Habiru and the Hebrews is to be found in the expressions "the gods of the Habiru" among the former, and "the God of the Hebrews" among the latter (Exodus 3:18; 5:3; etc.). When the Habiru entered into an agreement with another party, "the gods of the Habiru" were sometimes invoked, together with the gods of the other parties, as divine witnesses. Since the term "Hebrew" did not become associated with a sovereign land any more than "Habiru," the expression "the God of the Hebrews" is perfectly analogous.

The Patriarchs in Canaan

Abraham and his immediate descendants and relatives, including his nephew Lot, led a career which was characteristic of those days. They constituted a seminomadic group which settled for a while in a convenient region among the

Semitic and non-Semitic (especially Hurrian and Hittite) people of the land, and then, as shepherds, artisans, and the like, went on to another region. The land of the Canaanites, southern Syria and Palestine, was eminently suited to such free movement at that time. About 1800 B.C. western Palestine and southern Syria were generally occupied by city-states, largely under Egyptian control. Because the lowlands had the best soil and water supply, the cities of Palestine were located mostly along the Mediterranean coastal plain, in the valley of Jezreel (Esdraelon), and in the valley of the Jordan.

Central Palestine, the hilly region between the Jordan Valley and the coastal plain, was only sporadically settled. Though ill suited for agriculture, it was inviting enough to nomads with sheep and goats to graze. And so it was to this hill country, and to the even emptier and drier Negeb below, that Abraham and his family tended. In the Hill Country the patriarchs were associated with such places as Mamre, Bethel, Shechem, and Dothan (Map II). It is now known archaeologically that these places existed in this period; as a matter of fact, it would seem that Mamre was employed as the place-name in Abraham's time only because the better known Hebron was not yet founded (about 1700 B.C.).

In the Negeb, Beersheba was the focal point, as it has remained ever since. In Abraham's time Sodom and Gomorrah and other towns in the Vale of Siddim, at the southern end of the Dead Sea, were flourishing, and archaeology supports the Biblical story of their catastrophic end.

The patriarchal seminomadic mode of life required a relatively simple social structure. The father was the head of the family. The sons and daughters, with their spouses and children, were all subject to the authority of the patriarch. By tribal law, the oldest son succeeded the father upon his death. The tribe lived from its herds and flocks and from the itinerant labor of its craftsmen members—for example, the smiths and musicians.

Two Egyptian sources reproduce extraordinarily well the social atmosphere breathed in Genesis. An Egyptian by the name of Sinuhe tells of his experiences in southern Syria and northern Palestine during the latter half of the twentieth century B.C. He relates, in the "Tale of Sinuhe," how an important Amorite ruler in Syria took him in and married him to his oldest daughter:

He set me at the head of his children. He married me to his eldest daughter. . . . He made me ruler of a tribe of the choicest of the country. Bread was made for me as daily fare, wine as daily provision, cooked meat and roast fowl, beside the wild beasts of the desert, for they hunted for me. . . . I spent many years [there], and my children grew up to be strong men, each man as the chief of his own tribe. The messenger who went north or who went south to the Residence City tarried with me, for I used to make everybody stop over. I gave water to the thirsty. I put him who strayed, [back] on the road. I rescued him who had been robbed. . . . Every foreign country against which I went forth, when I had made my attack on it, was driven away from its pasturage and its wells. I plundered its cattle, carried off its inhabitants, took away their food, and slew people in it.[4]

The other Egyptian source is pictorial. A scene painted about 1900 B.C. on the wall of a noble's tomb at Beni Hasan, on the Nile in Middle Egypt, depicts a family of thirty-seven Semites from western Asia, seminomads come to Egypt to

[4] "The Story of Sinuhe," trans. J. A. Wilson, in *Ancient Near Eastern Texts relating to the Old Testament*, ed. J. B. Pritchard (Princeton, 1950), pp. 18–22.

sell stibium, the popular black eye cosmetic. Several elements in the scene are common to the Biblical material. One is reminded of the families of the patriarchs; Jacob's family which went down to Egypt numbered seventy persons, including the children and grandchildren. The clothes are striped lengthwise and very colorful, and recall Joseph's so-called "coat of many colors." The lyre, the javelins, the bows and arrows, and the portable bellows are all characteristic of the occupations of the seminomadic groups. The little donkeys in the scene were the principal means of travel before the domestication of the camel.

The Biblical and the archaeological data dovetail so well in this picture of the patriarchal period that one authority has been moved to say that the "Hebrew national tradition excels all others in its clear picture of tribal and family origins. In Egypt and Babylonia, in Assyria and Phoenicia, in Greece and Rome, we look in vain for anything comparable. There is nothing like it in the tradition of the Germanic peoples. Neither India nor China can produce anything similar." [5]

The Biblical Cosmogony

All religions have a cosmogony, an explanation of how the world and mankind came to be. The Biblical cosmogony in the Book of Genesis (Chapters 1–11), dealing with Creation, the Garden of Eden (Paradise), the Fall of Man, the antediluvian (pre-Flood) patriarchs, the Flood and Noah's Ark, the Tower of Babel and the dispersion of man over the earth—all these came from the earlier part of the second

---

[5] W. F. Albright, "The Biblical Period," in *The Jews: Their History, Culture and Religion,* ed. L. Finkelstein (New York, 1949), I, 3.

millennium, when the Hebrews had direct contact with Mesopotamian society. A relationship between the most important Babylonian story of creation, now popularly designated from its first two words, *Enûma Elish* ("When Above"), and the Biblical Genesis has long been recognized. Thus the two share in common the concept of a primeval watery chaos and the subsequent creation of the heaven and the earth. Both accounts speak of the existence of light prior to the creation of the sun, the moon, and the other heavenly bodies, which, in turn, made possible the regulation of time.

The Babylonian and the Hebrew versions both regard man as the final and most important act of creation, after which the creators rested. The Bible (Genesis 5) records ten patriarchs from Adam through Noah, who lived a total of 8,575 years, although the actual elapsed time was just over 1,000 years. Methuselah died at the ripest old age of them all, in his 969th year. Yet even these high numbers pale into insignificance in the light of one Sumerian list, which tells of eight antediluvian kings who reigned a total of 241,200 years, and a Babylonian list, compiled in the third century B.C. from much older sources, which records ten such rulers who reigned a total of 432,000 years.

The Biblical account of the Flood, with which God destroyed a world grown wicked, saving only enough of it to make a fresh start, is powerfully foreshadowed in the famous Gilgamesh Epic, which came down to the Babylonians from the earlier Sumerian civilization. Warned by the god Ea, Utnapishtim, the tenth antediluvian king in Babylonia, builds an ark in the shape of a cube, 120 cubits on each side. Into this ship he loads his family, his possessions, and "the seed of all living creatures." The epic relates how

Six days and nights
The wind blew, the downpour, the tempest, the flood over-
    whelmed the land,
When the seventh day arrived, the tempest, the flood,
Which had fought like an army, subsided in its onslaught.
The sea grew quiet, the storm abated, the flood ceased.
I opened a window, and light fell upon my face.
I looked upon the sea, (all) was silence,
And all mankind had turned to clay.

   . . . . .

On Mount Nisir (or Nimush) the ship landed.
Mount Nisir held the ship fast, and did not let it move.

   . . . . .

When the seventh day arrived,
I sent forth a dove and let her go.
The dove went away and came back to me;
There was no resting-place, and so she returned.
I sent forth a swallow and let her go.
The swallow went away and came back to me;
There was no resting-place, and so she returned.
I sent forth a raven and let her go.
The raven went away, and when she saw that the waters had
    abated,
She ate, she flew about, she cawed, and did not return.
I sent forth (everything) to the four winds and offered a
    sacrifice.
I poured out a libation on the peak of the mountain.[6]

Although the resemblances between the Gilgamesh Epic
and the Biblical account of Noah—who is also the tenth
antediluvian patriarch—are numerous and varied, including

---

[6] A. Heidel, *The Gilgamesh Epic and Old Testament Parallels*
(Chicago, 1946), pp. 81 ff.

such details as the Ark, the Flood, and the like, the differences are no less notable. It is frequently difficult to determine precisely what concepts the Hebrews derived from the various milieus in which they found themselves before about 1500 B.C. What is fundamental, however, is that the Hebrews infused whatever concepts they did borrow with their own spirit and thinking, thus endowing them with a content of ethics and morals which lifted the crass mythology of their Asiatic neighbors to a wholly new spiritual level.

The moral emphasis achieved in the Biblical cosmogony, as contrasted with the naturalism of the prototypes, is sharply illustrated by yet another Babylonian flood legend, the Atrakhasis Epic. Here we are told how

The god [Enlil] became disturbed by their gatherings.
The god heard their noise
And said to the great gods:
"Great has become the noise of mankind;
With their tumult they make sleep impossible."

In other words, the gods are moved to reprisal by simple personal annoyance, whereas in Genesis God's anger is stirred by man's moral decline. As the Bible says: "The Lord saw that the wickedness of man was great in the earth, and that every imagination of the thoughts of his heart was only evil continually" (Genesis 6:5).

The Patriarchal Conception of God and the Covenant

Some features in the patriarchal stage of Israelite history stand out with especial significance. While the picture in detail is still far from clear, the Biblical and the newer

archaeological data combine to indicate that the patriarchs
practiced a religion which, while not monotheistic in our
sense of the term, was yet not polytheistic either.

Its basic concept, later to develop into national significance, was the "covenant." This was the tribal practice of
entering into an agreement with one particular god, so that
the deity would devote himself entirely to the covenanters,
in return for their exclusive obedience and loyal trust. Abraham entered into a mutually exclusive agreement with God,
"the God of Abraham," whereby Abraham was to recognize and worship no other deity and God was to protect
and seek the welfare of Abraham and his family exclusively.

When Isaac renewed Abraham's covenant, God became
"the Kinsman of Isaac." For Jacob, God was "the Champion
of Jacob." Abraham's brother, Nahor, the one left behind
in Haran, likewise adopted a personal god. When Abraham's grandson Jacob and Nahor's grandson Laban settled
a dispute between themselves, Jacob said to Laban, "If the
God of my father, the God of Abraham and the Kinsman
of Isaac, had not been with me, you would have sent me
away empty" (Genesis 31:42). Whereupon Laban an-
swered, "Let the God of Abraham and the God of Nahor,
the God of their father, judge between us" (verse 53).

It would be going too far to attribute to the patriarchal
Hebrews a belief in the existence of one and only one God.
In a sense they may be said to have practiced—but without defining—monotheism. While they probably did not
think of denying the existence of other gods, and some
mighty ones among them at that, the patriarchs attached
themselves to one God, and Him alone they worshiped.
With Him, they entered voluntarily into a covenant which
was binding forever, never to be broken under penalty of

severe punishment and, theoretically at least, even complete rejection. It is not possible to understand the subsequent career of Israel without understanding these two inseparable concepts which arose in patriarchal times: practical monotheism and the personal covenant between the patriarchal families and their God.

The Questioning Spirit

Another phenomenon which apparently struck root in the patriarchal period is the fundamentally questioning and antidogmatic character and outlook of ancient Israel. It is true that within the patriarchal structure, the patriarch was the chief figure, and no one was free from his final authority. In actual life, however, the matriarch too was a dominant figure, for example, Abraham's wife Sarah and Isaac's wife Rebekkah. And within the household at large there was considerable freedom of action. In the domestic sphere, the woman's ameliorative counsels and her motherly feelings were taken seriously. An important check on patriarchal authority was economically grounded. By custom, the land was regarded as ultimately inalienable, so that family and tribal rather than private rights were the norm.

God, too, was conceived in patriarchal terms, theoretically omnipotent but actually subject to considerable questioning. He was not regarded as a faraway, impersonal deity. The very notion of a covenant implies the equality of the covenanters, and the devotion exacted from God by the patriarchs was no less thorough than that exacted from them by Him. He was near at hand whenever needed, a member of the patriarchal household and available for extended question-and-answer periods. Beginning with the seminomadic family structure of patriarchal society, and down to the time of the composition of the latest books in the Bible, there runs through Hebrew literature the characteristic and persistent feature of questioning authority. The Hebrew mind expressed its deepest self in its opposition to the absolute rule of any one man or tribe, be it kinsman or alien. This attitude extended even to the rule of God. Thus, in the famous dialogue between Abraham and God in Genesis 18:16–33, Abraham flatly objected when God proposed to obliterate Sodom, on the grounds that it was not fair to punish good men along with the bad. And Abraham would not rest content until God promised not to vent His anger, so long as there were as few as ten righteous men left. Which, however, seems not to have been the case.

The Book of Job provides an even more famous example of putting God to the question. But it is worth noting that neither Abraham nor Job partook of the character of a Promethean rebel. They were not insurrectionaries against God; they wanted only to see justice done, to understand and define God's powers, to have the contract properly drawn up and fulfilled on both sides.

CHAPTER II

Bondage, Exodus,

and the National Covenant⁓⁓⁓

THE SECOND important epoch in the career of ancient
Israel began with the descent of a group of Hebrews into
Egypt sometime around the late seventeenth or early sixteenth century B.C. By the time their descendants had found
their way back to Canaan, several centuries later, they were
on the verge of nationhood. The Egyptian experience was a
decisive factor in the development of Israel as a people.
Here the Hebrew families grew in number, and their con-
ception of God and His covenant with them was extended
to cover the entire Hebrew folk. Here also they continued
to oppose state autocracy, in contrast to the spineless submission of the Egyptian people at large. The ancient custom
of deifying kings, nowhere more elaborately developed
than in Egypt, left them fundamentally untouched. In this
great episode, the heroic figure of Moses stands out in epic
grandeur.

Eisodus: Egypt and the Hyksos

Whenever a drought and famine desolated the region of
Palestine, it was common for whole tribes to pick up their

belongings and seek refuge in Egypt. There the periodic overflow of the Nile gave life to the land, as it does today, and helped to regulate the agriculture of the country. The Egyptians learned early to dig channels for the seasonal flood and to irrigate the grain-producing land. Migration into Egypt was therefore an ancient expedient.

In Palestine, on the other hand, the rains did not always come when needed. A late-thirteenth-century Egyptian document, for example, tells how the seminomadic inhabitants of Edom, south of Palestine, left their homes in time of drought to come to Egypt "to keep themselves alive and to keep their cattle alive." It was famine, too, as the Bible says, which compelled Abraham and Isaac in an earlier period to go south (Genesis 12 and 26), and the same reason is given for Jacob's sending his sons to Egypt, where grain could still be procured even in a time of general drought (Genesis 42 ff.). As a result of this mission, the entire family finally settled there.

At the same time, this Eisodus—a "going into," as distinguished from the Exodus, a "going out of"—may also have been encouraged by certain ethnic disturbances which for a period disrupted Egyptian suzerainty in Canaan and reduced the sovereignty of the Egyptian homeland as well. Following upon the increasing disintegration of the Egyptian state, a mixed group of Asiatics, apparently mostly Semites, and known generally as Hyksos (literally, "rulers of foreign countries"), appeared in the north and swarmed down through Syria and Palestine. By about 1720 B.C. they had crossed the land bridge into Africa and conquered much of Egypt, a domination that was not to be completely broken until about 1550.

Between the Hyksos and the Hebrews there appear to

be a number of points of contact. It is known, for instance, that a certain Hyksos chieftain in Egypt bore the name Jacob-el, or perhaps Jacob-har, which means "May El, or Har [the mountain god] Give Protection." Another Hyksos leader was called Jacob-baal, "May Baal Protect." The verbal element, Jacob, which means "protect," is identical with the name of the Hebrew patriarch Jacob who settled in Egypt. Again, the historical kernel which resides in the dramatic story of the career of Joseph in Egypt, of the coming to power of a Hebrew in the Egyptian court, could well have derived from the period of the Hyksos, when Semites, and in all probability Habiru among them, were prominent among the new rulers of Egypt. For it was not Egyptian habit to nourish the ambitions of strangers in their midst. Furthermore, it would seem to be more than a mere coincidence that the Hebrews, according to the Bible, settled in Goshen in the Delta, the very area which the Hyksos built up around their new capital Avaris, the later Tanis.

In this connection it is also interesting to note that Josephus, the Jewish historian of the first century A.D., quotes the Egyptian historian Manetho (about 275 B.C.), to the effect that a large number of Hyksos made their way from Avaris to Canaan and there built Jerusalem. These Hyksos, according to Manetho, were "not fewer in number than 240,000," [1] a figure which recalls the Biblical statement (Numbers 1:46) that 603,550 Hebrew males, exclusive of Levites, women, and children, participated in the Exodus from Egypt.

All these facts suggest that the Hebrews and the Hyksos

[1] *Against Apion*, I, 14, ed. H. St. J. Thackeray, in *Loeb Classical Library* (New York, 1926).

may have been on terms of considerable intimacy; so that the entry of the Hebrews into Egypt would have been facilitated by the presence of Hyksos in positions of power, and the Bondage accounted for by the enslavement of foreign elements after the fall of the Hyksos invaders. If this hypothesis be accepted, it provides evidence that the Biblical version of the Hebrew sojourn in Egypt (Genesis 39–50; Exodus 1 ff.) derives from the same period as the events which it describes. For the Egyptians themselves, humiliated by their conquest at the hands of the Hyksos, avoided and suppressed any reference to the events of the period, and it would have been well-nigh impossible for anyone to learn the historical details very much later.

The Sojourn

The Bible itself elaborates only on the final period of the Bondage in Egypt. But what was there to say? After the Egyptians had overthrown the Hyksos, they enslaved those foreigners who had not fled, thus reversing the status of the non-Egyptians in the land as the Bible records: "And a new king arose in Egypt who did not know Joseph. . . . And they [the Egyptians] set taskmasters over them [the Hebrews] to afflict them with forced labor. And they built for Pharaoh store-cities, Pithom and Ramses" (Exodus 1:8–11).

Under the Hyksos domination, Egyptian culture had sunk so low that the period has been described as "The Great Humiliation." But the successful war of liberation against the Hyksos led to an Egyptian revival on such a grand scale that the period of the New Kingdom which followed, especially during the Eighteenth and Nineteenth Dynasties (about 1550–1150), has been called the Golden Age and was the subject of a recent book which bore the suggestive title, *When Egypt Ruled the East*.[2] The development of literature, art, and building, the inculcation of individual physical prowess in sport and in battle, the marked extension of the influence of women in the royal court and in upper-class circles generally—all of these manifested a new cosmopolitanism, and even secularism, brought on by imperial expansion abroad and urbanization at home.

There was much in the Egyptian environment that the Hebrews could emulate. But the kind of life which they and others led in the Egyptian slave camps did not encourage cultural apprenticeship. "Slave troops on a government building project," as one authority puts it, "have no opportunity for discussion with priests and scribes. Their simple desert souls would see and shrink from some of the abominations of the effete civilization and long to escape dreary enslavement rather than admire the cultural triumph of the land of bondage." [3]

Moses, Leader of the Exodus

It was probably sometime in the thirteenth century that a group of Hebrews and others united under the leadership of Moses, of the tribe of Levi, to escape from Egypt. This tribe was foremost in organizing those state slaves who were willing to chance the break for freedom. Several outstanding Levites bore Egyptian names, for example, Moses, Miriam, Hophni, Phinehas, Merari, Puti-el, and perhaps Aaron. This alone indicates a considerable period of residence in Egypt; also a surprising degree of resistance and determination to be free, despite a long period of slavery.

[2] G. Steindorff and K. C. Seele, *When Egypt Ruled the East* (Chicago, 1942).

[3] J. A. Wilson, *The Burden of Egypt* (Chicago, 1951), p. 256.

The Bible makes it amply clear that many non-Hebrew elements, "the mixed multitude" of Exodus (12:38) and Numbers (11:4), accompanied Moses and the Hebrews out of Egypt. The Egyptian sources, in turn, provide a very clear background for this circumstance. Tens of thousands of workers, natives of many countries and members of different ethnic groups, labored for the Egyptian state. Already in the fifteenth century, as a result of the military conquests of Amenhotep II in Syria and Palestine, large numbers of Semitic and non-Semitic captives of war, including 3,600 Apiru (Habiru), were brought to Egypt as state slaves. The military campaigns of other Egyptian kings, from the fourteenth to the twelfth centuries, produced similar results. The great building projects of Ramses II (about 1301–1234), at such places as Pithom and Ramses, employed these "mixed multitudes," many of whom were eager to escape from slavery.

Scholars have long been troubled by the fact that Egyptian records make no mention of Moses and the Exodus, and some have expressed the belief that a document or two may yet turn up with reference to them. Yet the modern student of ancient Egyptian history should share neither this worry nor this optimism. First, when the Egyptians lost a battle, they customarily either recorded it as a victory or else passed over it in silence. Thus the prolonged Hyksos rule was not mentioned in contemporaneous Egyptian sources until the Hyksos were expelled, and even the victory over them was apparently not officially recorded. And second, the scope of the Exodus and the significance of it for the Egyptian government were so meager as not to merit any documentary mention.

The Wandering in the Wilderness

The peninsula of Sinai is a smaller replica of the Arabian peninsula, which lies farther east and south of it. On the west, Sinai is bounded by a deep-reaching arm of the Red Sea, and on the east by the Gulf of Aqabah, as the Persian Gulf forms the eastern bound of the Arabian peninsula. It was into this burning desert upland that Moses led the way.

Here, in the wilderness of Sinai, Israel was forged, hammered into shape amid appalling hardship. The weak and weary perished, leaving the young and strong to drift yet another mile toward the Land of Promise, the ancestral home.

There was endless and violent struggle for power within this group that Moses had led from Egypt. Korah and his faction of Levites and Reubenites challenged the authority of Moses himself (Numbers 16). Aaron, in the incident of the Golden Calf, was used by another faction in a similar struggle (Exodus 32). There was the additional difficulty that the "mixed multitude" reminded themselves in the wilderness of Sinai of "the flesh which we used to eat in Egypt free; the cucumbers, and the melons, and the leeks, and the onions and the garlic; but now our strength is dried up" (Numbers 11:4–5). Only a man of iron will could have endured this endless bickering, scheming, and back-sliding. Moses was that man.

It was in the wilderness of Sinai, and not in Egypt or Canaan, that this struggle for power took place, and the subsequent welding together of a heterogeneous, inexperienced, and uncultured mass of individuals into something of a unified force and social group. That about a generation —the traditional "forty years" of wandering—should have elapsed before the goal was approached is not only reasonable, but also accounts for the fact that virtually none of the leaders of the Exodus, such as Moses, Aaron, and Miriam, lived to enter the Promised Land.

Until recently the Bible has been virtually the only source for the history of the wandering in the Wilderness. As a result, the significance of this stage in Israel's history has been minimized, when its very authenticity has not been questioned.

A central feature of the Biblical account is the movable Tabernacle, or Tent of Meeting, around which the political and religious life of the wandering Hebrews revolved. This institution used to be regarded as a late fiction, projected back into the past. Recently, however, archaeological and literary parallels have been accumulating which not only explain the origin of this structure and institution in the wilderness of Sinai, but also clarify its history as the "Tent of the Lord" at Shiloh, following the conquest of Canaan. It was ultimately replaced by the Temple which David planned and Solomon built.

Much the same thing happened in the case of the Ark, the acacia chest in which, according to tradition, Moses placed and kept the two stone tablets recording the Ten Commandments. Furthermore, the traditional route of the Wandering, as described in the books of Exodus and Numbers, accords well with the topography of Sinai and with what has been learned of the location of the copper and turquoise mines which were being worked and garrisoned in the thirteenth century B.C. These garrisoned sites, in the hands of the Egyptians, appear to have been situated at just those points which the Hebrews were careful to avoid in their trek through Sinai.[4]

Moses and the Covenant

The Covenant between God and the new nation, a factor of fundamental importance in Israel's career, came into being during this period. The relationship between the patriarchs and their God had begun, according to the social patterns of seminomadic family life, as a personal arrangement. In Moses' first experience with the Deity, at the theophany in the burning bush (Exodus 3), the relationship was also personal; and in accord with the patriarchal tradition, the Deity Himself acquired a new personal name, YHWH, which is usually rendered "Lord" or "Jehovah." [5]

The experiences of the Exodus and the Wandering gradually forged the more individualistic elements into the new tribal or national unit. The purpose of the Exodus was not merely to free a group of slaves for their own sake, but for

[4] F. M. Cross, Jr., "The Tabernacle," *Biblical Archaeologist*, X (Sept., 1947), 45–68.

[5] The Hebrew term consists of four letters, YHWH, and hence is called the Tetragrammaton. Some time after about the fifth century B.C., the original pronunciation of the name ceased to be employed for ordinary purposes, and the term Adonai, "Lord," came to be substituted for it. The term Jehovah is a relatively recent creation (about fourteenth century A.D.), by a Christian who erroneously read the vowels of Adonai together with the consonants of YHWH. The Revised Standard Version (New York, 1952) follows the tradition of the King James (so-called Authorized) Version, the Revised Version, and the Jewish Publication Society Translation in rejecting the term Jehovah, usually in favor of LORD.

Many scholars believe that the original pronunciation of YHWH was Yahweh. The evidence for this belief, however, is not decisive, and there are also very considerable differences of opinion as to what the term meant originally.

something far greater in scope and significance, the creation of a new nation. The direct relationship between God and the Nation was the new element created by the forces of history and circumstance. From that point on, and throughout the entire Bible henceforth, the new Covenant, a national pact between God and His people, sealed by the act of the Exodus, replaced the older, individual covenants between God and the patriarchal leaders.

The personality of Moses so dominated Israel's formative years that later centuries came to credit him with authorship of the Pentateuch. This honor is more than justified in a figurative sense, and to some extent in a factual sense as well. Research has now shown that an important part of the legal code of ancient Israel clearly derives from the pre-Canaanite period which coincides with the Hebrew wandering in the Wilderness (see below in Chapter III). And the Sinaitic origin of the Tabernacle, noted above, implies the development of numerous religious and cultic regulations under the leadership of Moses.

Great intelligence and character were required to solve the many vexing problems, to take advantage fully and wisely of the new and changing circumstances, to know when to follow and when to lead the unorganized Hebrews and their fellow travelers. When the mixed tribal following had emerged from the wilderness, they were all bound to one God. Moses alone provided that essential leadership, and he well deserves his traditional reputation of having brought Israel into being as a nation.

The question of who would succeed Moses in authority was of prime importance; there appears to have been no opposition to Moses' selection of Joshua of the tribe of Ephraim as his successor.

Moses and the Atonism of Akh-en-aton

According to a much-quoted theory, Moses could have acquired the concept of monotheism which he introduced to the Hebrews only from the Egyptian environment in which he had grown up, specifically from the so-called monotheism of the Aton. This worship of the round disk of the sun, while known previously in Egypt, found an ardent devotee in Amenhotep IV (Akh-en-aton; about 1380–1362 B.C.).

Two important facts, however, each independent of the other, disprove this theory. First, in sponsoring monotheism, Moses was actually not introducing a new concept to the Hebrews. He had a familiar, developable Hebraic idea of monotheism to work with, and there was nothing fundamental in his approach to the Deity which was not already to be found in the patriarchal period. Even the Covenant of Sinai represented not so much a change in kind as a change in degree from the old way of binding oneself to the Deity. Second, Moses could hardly have been affected by Atonism, since this worship was limited to Akh-en-aton and his family and was crushed immediately after Akh-en-aton's death. Indeed, Akh-en-aton's own courtiers had worshiped Akh-en-aton himself. Finally, Atonism itself was not truly monotheistic.

J. A. Wilson has recently declared: "As to whether Atonism was ancestral to Hebrew monotheism . . . it may be stated flatly that the mechanism of transmission from the faith of Akh-en-aton to the monotheism of Moses is not apparent. This was the personal religion of a Pharaoh who later became a heretic within one generation. . . ." [6] In

[6] Wilson, *op. cit.*, pp. 224 ff.

general, the Bible makes it clear that the Hebrews brought
with them from Egypt little or no cultural baggage; while
from the Egyptian side the question is well summed up in
the statement, "Our argument then is that there certainly
were bondages and that there certainly was an exodus, but
that neither of these experiences was an effective instrument for cultural transmission, but was rather a barrier to
such transmission." [7]

[7] *Ibid.*, p. 256.

Israel in Canaan:

The Period of the Judges

CANAAN was the home of the patriarchs, and it was with this land that the God of the patriarchs was associated. Moses and all later leaders recognized this fundamental fact, and it was to Canaan that they led the Hebrews through the wilderness. During the period of the Judges, in the twelfth and eleventh centuries, the term "Israelites" replaced that of "Hebrews," and the relationship of God, Israel, and the Land of Israel became intertwined and indissoluble, as it has remained ever after. In the view of the Biblical writers there could have been no Israel without God and the Holy Land.

The Geography of the Land of Israel

Palestine covers approximately 10,000 square miles spread over an area that stretches from Dan in the north, at the foot of the Anti-Lebanon mountain range, to below Beersheba in the south, and from the Mediterranean Sea in the west to the desert fringes of Transjordan in the east. (See Map II.) The whole territory, of which about three-fifths lies west of the Jordan, resembles in size and shape the state

II. Israel in the period of the judges and kings (about 1200–600 B.C.).

of New Hampshire, the forty-third state in area in the Union. This little country is broken up into some eight natural geographical units.

First there is the coastal plain along the Mediterranean, about ten miles wide and divided in half approximately at Joppa, near modern Tel Aviv. The Plain of Sharon lies to the north as far as the Carmel range near modern Haifa, and the more important Philistine plain, Philistia, lies to the south. The Plain of Acco extends north of Sharon, from the Carmel mountains to Acco and somewhat beyond. Further along the coast lay Phoenicia, separated from Acco and the rest of western Palestine by mountains of the region.

To the east of and paralleling Philistia rises the Shefelah, the second principal area, which is separated by longitudinal valleys from the central Hill Country and forms the transition to it. The Hill Country begins in southern Syria and in the form of hills and mountains extends down the length of Palestine until it begins to peter out in the extreme south.

The third part, the northern Hill Country, is called Galilee, and is usually subdivided into Upper and Lower Galilee. The fourth unit is the Valley of Jezreel, or Esdraelon (or simply "The Valley"), which cuts right across Galilee and constitutes the easy road for traders and invaders to reach Transjordan. Central Palestine, the fifth part, consisted of Samaria in the north, with the southern sector constituting Judah. The sixth division, formed by the rest of western Palestine, was the vast semiarid area in the south, the Negeb.

The territory west of the Jordan, the seventh section, was separated from Transjordan by a geologically marvellous "rift valley," the corollary of the long range of hills which forms the Hill Country. This rift begins in Syria, separates and forms Mount Lebanon and Mount Anti-Lebanon (Biblical Hermon), and continues south in the form of the Jordan Valley and the Arabah, to the Gulf of Aqabah and the Red Sea—indeed, as far as Mozambique and into the great depressions filled by the African lakes. The Jordan River runs through the valley, pooled en route in Lake Huleh (approximately the Waters of Merom) and the Sea of Galilee (or Chinnereth), and terminates to the south in the *cul-de-sac* which is the Dead, or Salt, Sea. All these bodies of water fill below-sea-level troughs in the valley floor. The Dead Sea, about 1,275 feet below the Mediterranean, is the lowest depression in the world.

Finally, eastern Palestine, or Transjordan, is essentially a plateau, and is divided up by four rivers into five main regions. The Yarmuk River, flowing into the Jordan just south of the Sea of Galilee, made up the dividing line between Bashan and Gilead. The Jabbok, or Wadi Zerqa, emptying into the Jordan about two-thirds of the way down, constituted the boundary between Gilead and Ammon. The Arnon, or Wadi Mojib, in turn, sometimes served as the natural barrier between Ammon and Moab, at the middle of the Dead Sea. The boundary between the two countries varied during Biblical times, usually lying north of the Arnon. Finally, at the southern end of the Dead Sea, the Zered, or Wadi Hesa, separated Moab from Edom. When it rained, these wadis became real streams. Otherwise they were mostly dry riverbeds.

The Climate of the Holy Land

Small as it is, Palestine has always had the advantages of many kinds of climate, owing in part to the variety of the terrain. In general, the land resembles the drier parts of Southern California, but everything is on a much smaller scale. Mount Hermon in the north, which is over 9,000 feet high, tends to be cold, whereas just over one hundred miles to the south, in the Jordan Valley, Jericho swelters in tropical heat. Jerusalem, although less than fifteen miles to the southwest of Jericho, is almost 4,000 feet higher, and its inhabitants have usually found its climate temperate.

From Jerusalem to the coast the distance is just over thirty miles, and the descent from about 2,600 feet to sea level. The coastal climate is of course much warmer, although never so unbearable in summer as the Jordan Valley. The temperatures in the Transjordan plateau approximate those of Jerusalem.

There is another important element, the winds. The winds from the east are usually hot and dry, coming as they do from the desert. Those from the north, on the other hand, and especially from the west across the Mediterranean, are much more gentle, bringing with them cool air and rain. The all-important rainy season usually begins in October and ends in March or April. One of God's greatest blessings to Israel was His promise: "I will give the rain of your land in its season, the former rain and the latter rain, that you may gather in your grain, and your wine, and your oil" (Deuteronomy 11:14; 28:12). The threat of drought was a curse and a disaster (28:23–24).

Geography and Economy

A network of valleys provided avenues of settlement as well as commercial and military traffic. This made for the historical interplay between hill and valley peoples that figures so prominently in the books of Joshua, Judges, and Samuel.

Geography made Biblical Israel primarily an agricultural, and only secondarily a commercial, society. The coastal plains of Sharon and Philistia, the Jezreel and Jordan valleys, and a considerable part of the Hill Country of Samaria and Judah lent themselves to successful farming. Even the nearly waterless Negeb was tilled profitably when the inhabitants diligently exploited the available supply of water by terracing and irrigating the land.

Ancient Israel, with its few and inadequate harbors, derived slight commercial advantage from its Mediterranean coast. Even Dor and Joppa, the nation's best ports, could be used only when the sea was calm. Such better harbors as were to be found along the coast, Byblos, Sidon, Tyre, and usually even Acco, were in Phoenician hands. In the days of Solomon, considerable maritime trade centered about Ezion-geber and Elath on the Gulf of Aqabah and continued at least sporadically for some time after his reign.

It was as the bridge between Asia and Africa that the land of Israel acquired commercial significance. Its plains and valleys, notably Jezreel and the Mediterranean coast, were commercial and military highways from time immemorial; and this fact explains why the sites which guarded and controlled these routes played so important a role in Biblical history. Beth-shan, Megiddo, Shechem, Gaza, and Beersheba were among the better-known cities in the west, and in Transjordan such sites as Ashtaroth, Ramoth-gilead, Rabbath-ammon, Heshbon, and Kir-hareseth dominated the main road from Damascus through Bashan, Gilead, Ammon, and Moab, to Edom in the south.

Israel was not rich in natural resources. The copper and

iron ores in the south were exploited by the Israelites only when Edom was under their control. Limited both in area and water supply, the country could not support a large population, but in spite of that the Israelites might well have succeeded in turning their domain into "a land flowing with milk and honey" (Exodus 3:8) if it had not fallen directly across the path of invasion and conquest followed by the expanding empires of western Asia and Egypt.

Joshua and the Conquest of Canaan: The Ideal and the Reality

According to the traditional understanding of the Biblical account, the taking of Canaan was accomplished in a single spectacularly successful invasion, with Joshua smiting one-and-thirty kings. In this picture, the Hebrew tribes, led by Joshua, crossed the Jordan near the Dead Sea and took the key point of Jericho, "whose walls came tumbling down." The next objective was Ai, up in the Hill Country, just over ten miles west of Jericho as the crow flies, but twice as far by foot. This fortified place Joshua took by strategem.

Thereafter, in a series of forays up the valleys—on one occasion, the lost Book of Jashar tells us (Joshua 10:12–14), he commanded the sun in Gibeon and the moon in the valley of Aijalon to stand still, so that he could mop up remnants of Canaanite resistance—Joshua took and razed a series of fortified towns, Libnah, Lachish, Eglon, Hebron, and Debir. This done, he conquered all the highland of southern Canaan, a section of the coastal strip as far as Gaza, and then in the north by the Waters of Merom, a hundred miles more or less from his base at Gilgal, he routed a Canaanite army.

Reuben, Gad, and half of the tribe of Manasseh took occupation of Transjordan; the other half of Manasseh settled on the Plain of Sharon just south of Esdraelon. The tribe of Levi, consisting entirely of religious functionaries, received no single fixed territory. The rest of the tribes shared in the partition of Canaan according to their population.

The author of Chapters 10–11 in the Book of Joshua provides the basis for this traditional view. Joshua, he recounts,

defeated all the land, the hill country, and the Negeb, and the Shefelah, and the slopes, and all their kings; he left none remaining, but utterly destroyed all that breathed . . . So Joshua took the whole land, according to all that the Lord said to Moses; and Joshua gave it for an inheritance to Israel according to their divisions by their tribes. And the land had rest from war.

Chapters 15–19 in Joshua and Chapter 1 in Judges, however, give a different picture both of the conquest and of the role of Joshua therein. This version describes the conquest as a slow piecemeal affair, accomplished largely after Joshua and his generation were gone, by individual tribes and clans seldom acting even in partial unison. Thus Judges 1: 1 would indicate that the land was not at rest from war, in fact was never pacified: "After the death of Joshua, the Israelites asked of the Lord, 'Who shall go up for us first against the Canaanites to fight against them?'"

The latter picture of the conquest was generally taken by scholars to be correct and the former thrown into discard, together with Joshua's traditional career, as myth. The truth of the matter, however, appears to comprehend both versions. Excavations at Lachish, Tell Beit Mirsim (= Kiriat-sepher?), Hebron, Eglon, Beth-shemesh, Gibeah, Bethel, Shiloh, Megiddo, and Beth-shan indicate that these places were destroyed or occupied, then were sometimes retaken and rebuilt by the Canaanites, only to change hands again, during the thirteenth, twelfth, and eleventh centuries B.C. The Biblical version of the Joshuan conquest would seem to be "a collection of miscellaneous fragments *of varying dates and of varying reliability* . . . There was a campaign by Joshua which achieved an amazing success in attacking certain key Canaanite royal cities but . . . there was also a long period of struggle for possession which continued after Joshua's death." [1]

Biblical authors tended to telescope accounts of long campaigns—a device by no means abandoned even today—and to give all the credit for victory to well-established military heroes such as Joshua. Their purpose, after all, was not merely to chronicle but to dramatize the past and to edify their readers. To achieve this end they naturally tended to lump weary details under one splendid name. Thus Joshua acquires once again an association with the conquest of Canaan no less deserving and prominent in its way than that of Moses with the Exodus and the Wilderness.

Hebrews and Israelites

During the Period of the Judges, the term "Israel" (or "Israelites") came to replace the term "Hebrew," just as the term "Israelites" was later replaced by "Judeans" and "Jews" after the Exile in Babylon (see Chapter VI). There is good historical reason for this change.

The term "Hebrew," according to the Bible, is older than "Israel." The latter, it will be remembered, originated with the superhuman being who, after wrestling all night

---

[1] Quoted from G. E. Wright, in *Journal of Near Eastern Studies,* V (1946), 105–114. Joshua's capture of Ai was probably confused with that of Bethel. The archaeological story of Jericho is not clear.

without being able to overcome him, bestowed it on Jacob
(Genesis 32:23–33). Outside the Bible, the term Habiru is
likewise found earlier than Israel, the latter occurring for
the first time in the extant literature about 1230 B.C., when
King Merneptah of Egypt celebrated victory over numerous foes in an alleged campaign in western Asia. The Pharaoh
boasted:

> Israel is laid waste, its seed is not,
> Palestine is become a widow for Egypt.

The origin of the terms "Israel" and "Hebrew," not to
mention the relationship between the two, is as obscure as
the history of the tribes which bore these names. The
fragmentary character of the Biblical data concerning this
problem permits little more than scholarly speculation; but
what does appear clear is that Biblical writers began to use
the term "Israelites" (literally, "the Children of Israel")
approximately when the Hebrews began to constitute a
nation, that is, at the time of the Exodus, Wandering, and
Conquest.

The last reference to the Hebrews as a distinct group
occurs in connection with the bitter struggle between the
Philistine hosts and the Israelite forces of King Saul (I Samuel 14:21 and 29:3). The Hebrew text (14:21) appears
to say that the Hebrews had sided with the Philistines and
were now deserting to the Israelites; but the text is really
not as clear as the English translations would make it appear.

The Canaanite Civilization

When the Hebrews and Israelites entered Canaan, they
found there a highly developed and sophisticated society.
Thanks to very recent discoveries of inscriptions and other

archaeological evidence, part of this highly significant culture has been recovered.[2] Indeed, the Canaanite civilization
was so advanced that it nearly absorbed the desert invaders.
Thus it was when the Semitic Akkadians swept into the
non-Semitic society of Sumer. Thus, too, when Rome conquered Greece, the victors were in turn conquered by the
superior culture of their victims.

There can be no doubt that the Israelites of Joshua and
Judges were quite unable to match the material techniques
of Canaan, at least until the period of Solomon in the tenth
century. Israelite fortifications, Saul's strong point at Gibeah
for example, did not compare with those of contemporary
Canaan. The foundations and masonry found in Canaanite
towns are clearly superior to Israelite remains. Canaanite
Bethel had a drainage system, which was unknown in Israelite towns. Canaanite pottery of the Middle and Late Bronze
Ages (about 2000–1200 B.C.) compared with the best, but
the products of Israel were crude.

The origin of the alphabet cannot as yet be determined
with precision. It is the Canaanites, however, who may well
have been associated with its invention, who gave this
great cultural force to the world at large. It is likewise uncertain exactly what Semitic language or languages the
Hebrews and Israelites spoke in the patriarchal period; but
after they settled in Canaan, they adopted a variety of
Canaanite alphabets and dialects. For good reason, then, the
Bible itself calls the Hebrew language "the tongue of Canaan" (Isaiah 19:18), recognizing Biblical Hebrew as originally a dialect of Canaanite.

[2] W. F. Albright, *The Archaeology of Palestine* (Pelican Books,
1949), chs. v and vi; C. H. Gordon, *Ugaritic Literature* (Rome,
1949).

Canaanite literature was notable for its mythological and religious compositions. The Greeks and Romans owed much more than their alphabet to the Canaanites, whom the Greeks began to call Phoenicians after about 1000 B.C.; they derived also considerable and important elements in their mythologies from them.

The religious system was a highly organized and central element in every aspect of the daily life of the Canaanites, and its influence extended widely into the economic, political, and social spheres. The priests constituted an important and powerful group in the upper class of Canaanite society. They were landowners, slaveowners, and money-lenders on a large scale, operating within the temples and under the protection of the gods. In Canaan, as in Mesopotamia and Egypt, the temples "were heavily endowed with landed properties and received a tremendous income. At certain periods they probably owned nearly all the land of the country and acquired almost an economic strangle-hold over the people." [3]

The religious beliefs and practices of the Canaanites revolved about the predominantly agricultural character of their economy. The Canaanites were polytheists, regarding the forces of nature as divine beings and giving to them personal names. These deities personified the heavenly bodies—the sun, moon, stars, and planets—and such manifestations of nature as rain, thunder, lightning, vegetation, death, and wisdom—the last mentioned including the arts and inventions.

Mythological stories and qualities were woven about the

[3] From a symposium on "The Significance of the Temple in the Ancient Near East," *The Biblical Archaeologist*, VII (Sept. and Dec., 1944), 41–88.

careers of the gods, and much of the ritual at the shrines of Canaanite cults was intended primarily to ensure the fertility of the soil. Foremost among the gods was Baal, to whom there is so much derogatory reference in the Bible. The Canaanite Baal was a god of rain, prime mover of the agricultural world. Periodically Baal was killed by the forces of Mot, the god of drought and death, so that the rains and vegetation ceased. However, Baal came to life in the fall, and the all-important rains came down again. In the spring Baal and his half-sister Anath, goddess of fertility and war, cohabited, so that fecundity came to the land and its inhabitants. The Canaanite worship of their gods was characterized by idolatry and sexual rites.[4]

Israel and Canaan

The manner in which the Israelites reacted to the Canaanite civilization forms one of the vivid periods in their dramatic career. It will be remembered that not all the Hebrews left Canaan for Egypt in the days of Jacob and Joseph. The stay-at-homes inclined to feel indifferent about a Bondage and Exodus in which their own ancestors had not participated. While their kinsmen had been off adventuring and finding God, they themselves had acquired land, herds, and status. And to this end they had compromised, in great measure or small, with the culture and religion of Canaan. Not for them the harsh dedications of the Law, the admonition from on high, "Be very strong and courageous, being mindful to do according to all the Law which Moses My servant commanded you. . . . This book of the Law shall not depart out of your mouth, but you shall meditate on it day and night . . . for then you shall make your way

[4] T. H. Gaster, *Thespis* (New York, 1950).

prosperous, and you shall have good success" (Joshua
1:7–8). These people had already feathered their nests without the assistance of the Covenant.

Among the new settlers too there developed different
points of view. Some of those fresh from the Mosaic scene,
once they were comfortably ensconced, found it desirable
to wink an eye and look away from the Law. On several
occasions the tribes of Reuben and Gad and the half-tribe
of Manasseh had to be ordered to help their fellow tribes-
men secure their allotments in western Palestine (Joshua
1:12–18). When the crucial struggle between the Israelites
and the Canaanites came to a head in the battle near Taanach
in the valley of Jezreel (about 1125 B.C.), an event made
famous by the triumphal Song of Deborah (Judges 5), several tribes refused to join in the battle and accordingly were
cursed. A whole century of indecision and wavering passed
before the reluctant tribes, faced with a common danger,
were able to bring themselves to make a common cause.
The individualism and desert ways of these tribes died hard.

The same process is reflected in the religious picture
painted in the Book of Judges. The complete devotion to
the Lord advocated by Moses and Joshua ran into dire opposition. The Israelite population at large, even the new-
comers in the land, conveniently adapted their way of life
to the Canaanite practices, especially those which were
aimed at the maintenance and improvement of their well-
being. Local shrines, with individual priestly families and
seers in charge, sprang up everywhere. While they did not
go so far as to produce idols to represent the Lord, many
Israelites did acquire figurines of the Canaanite goddess of
fertility. They also added to the worship of the Lord

ritualistic features from the cults of Baal, Asherah, Ash-toreth, and the other gods of Canaan. In spite of this, the God of Israel survived through thick and thin, even when His influence was diluted by alien admixture. Such heroes as Saul and David (about 1000 B.C.), it should be noted, gave some of their children names which included the element "Baal."

But some, the Gideons of Israel, would not take the pagan bait. At the behest of the Lord, the Bible tells us in Judges 6, Gideon risked his life in the dark of the night by smashing a Baal altar and cutting down the Asherah beside it for firewood for burning an Israelite sacrificial bull. "And when the men of the town rose early in the morning," the account continues, "behold, the altar of Baal was broken down, and the Asherah was cut down that was by it, and the second bull was offered [to the Lord] upon the altar which had been built" (verse 26).

The authors of the Book of Judges openly blamed Israel's misfortunes during the period of settlement upon this widespread religious defection. When Midianite camel raiders and the better-organized forces of Ammon and Moab overran Israelite communities, their depredations were explained as punishment for Israel's desertion of the Lord. Israel would not have experienced these sufferings, the Biblical writers maintained (Judges 2:11 ff.), if she had held together under the Covenant. Israel's strength lay in united devotion to the Lord, and the worship of Baal was the most divisive and destructive force that Israel had to face. It threatened to destroy the Covenant between God and His chosen people.

The Judges

The period from Joshua to King Saul is described in the Bible as "the days when the judges ruled." These "judges" were primarily local military heroes and dominated Israel during the period of pacification and adjustment. When an alien force attacked a segment of Israel, men of uncommon mettle frequently stepped forward from among the people to rally and lead their fellows. Such natural leaders, if they proved successful, became judges and were accepted as rulers within the area of resistance (Judges 2:14 ff.).

The Bible records some twelve judges in all, some of them contemporaries, as in the case of Ehud and Shamgar. The most famous judges were Ehud, Gideon, Jephthah, and Samson. These successful military chieftains acquired judicial authority, alongside the priests of the local sanctuaries, but only secondarily, and they held it only so long as "the land had rest" from the enemy. Unlike the judges of the later monarchy, these judges were brought into being by external, military needs.

Not more than three leaders in the Period of the Judges really adjudicated; they were Deborah, Eli, and Samuel. Eli, however, was specifically a priest. And Deborah and Samuel, unlike the others, are described as "prophets"; indeed, neither one ever served as military leader for any of the tribes.

Tribal Structure of Israel and her Neighbors

Except for occasional brief emergency alliances, the Israelite tribes maintained complete autonomy during the Period of the Judges and recognized no central capital or shrine for all Israel. "In those days there was no king in

Israel, every man did what was right in his own eyes"
(Judges 17:6; 21:25). The hilly terrain, netted by a maze
of valleys and wadis, made for political disjunction. Since
no enemy was powerful enough to threaten more than a
small part of Israel at any one time, the pressure from
without was not great enough to produce any effective
integration.

The Canaanite society, moreover, consisted of independent fortified townships without any tradition of commonwealth or of mutual assistance. Canaanite political example,
if anything, tended to retard the development of the na-
tionalism latent in the Mosaic Covenant. The authority of
the Canaanites was undermined, in any case, by their pagan-
ism. Customs both old and new thus militated against unity
among the Israelite tribes. Dwellers on the plains ignored
the plight of the hill people, who returned the compliment.
And intertribal warfare itself was not unknown, despite
a common religion (Judges 12:19–21).

Across the valley, on the Transjordan plateau, lived other
Semitic peoples, in all probability of the same Habiru origin
as the Israelites. If the Biblical account is taken literally,
at least one of these countries was a monarchy. "And these
are the kings that reigned in the land of Edom," the Scriptures tell us, "before there reigned any king over the children of Israel" (Genesis 36:31–39; I Chronicles 1:43–51).
Whereupon eight kings are listed.

It appears that the Edomite term "king" meant something
essentially different from what it came to mean later on,
since none of these "kings" was ever succeeded by a son or
by any relative or even any fellow townsman. As a matter
of fact, the Edomite kings are listed in the same manner as
the local chieftains in the above-mentioned chapters in

Genesis and Chronicles and exactly like the list of judges in
Judges 10:1–3 and 12:8–15. It would seem that an Edomite
"king" was about the same sort of personage as "King"
Abimelech of Shechem, son of Gideon the Judge (Judges
9). In other words, he was a mere chieftain with extraordinary powers of a provisional and local nature.

Nor did the Ammonites or the Moabites, any more than
the Edomites, have a centralized form of government at
the time of the judges. If the Ammonites could not overcome the small forces of Jephthah (Judges 11), and if Ammon, Moab, and Amalek had to combine to establish power
even in a small part of Israel (Judges 3), and if Israel, in
turn, could dominate Moab, it is extremely unlikely that
any of these Transjordanian territories was monarchized
or, by virtue of a central government, capable of present-
ing a united front. But soon events came to pass which
corrected this irregular situation.

Israelite Economy and Government

The Israelites, meanwhile, raised cattle, sheep, and goats
and tilled the soil. Artisans organized guilds, practiced weav-
ing, dyeing, tanning, smithing, pottery making, and other
crafts, even though on a very small scale.[5] Private ownership of land, including wells, gradually replaced the com-
munal ownership of patriarchal days.

Even though there was a concentration of wealth among
the Canaanites, rich families among the Israelites did not

[5] See in general M. S. and J. L. Miller, *Encyclopedia of Bible Life*
(New York, 1944), chs. v and xvii. The Jewish Palestine (now,
Israel) Exploration Society issued in 1937, as Vols. IX–X in its excellent *Library of Palestinology* (in Hebrew), ed. S. Yeivin, a useful
treatment of *Trade, Industry and Crafts in Ancient Palestine*, by
various authors.

appear to dominate the communities in the time of the judges. Imposing palaces and elaborate fortifications discovered in the Canaanite levels of Palestinian mounds are not equaled in the Israelite levels until the days of Solomon. The lack of concentrated wealth also helped hold back the development of a nationally conscious leadership. This circumstance accounts also for the absence from Israel, at least up to the time of David, of the *corvée*, or forced labor.

It would seem that during the Period of the Judges a form of primitive democracy functioned among the Israelites. There does not appear to have been any centralized authority within the tribal unit capable of dominating the rest of the population. The heads of wealthy and important families constituted a group of "elders," and they met— usually in the town gate, the common meeting place in those days—whenever the occasion demanded. In conjunction with the elders, although the precise relationship remains obscure, there also functioned a public assembly of all the free adult males of the community. The elders and the assembly made their authority felt in every aspect of the community's activities, the military, political, religious, economic, legal, and social. In Israelite society it was not easy to separate the religious from the secular aspects of these activities.

Israel's Legal Codes

During the Period of the Judges the legal system of Israel began to take on definite shape. It is now generally agreed that the legal enactments in the Pentateuch fall into two main groups. Numerous laws are introduced by a direct command or prohibition of the Lord, "You shall (or, shall not). . . ." The Ten Commandments (Exodus 20:1–17)

are a case in point, e.g., "You shall not have any other gods
before Me," etc. Laws expressed so dogmatically and directly are called *apodictic*.

The second major group of laws, called *casuistic*, is characterized by a conditional clause ("if; provided that"). The
Book of the Covenant (Exodus 20:22–23:33; 24:7) is a good
example of this formulation, e.g., "If a thief be found break-
ing in, and be smitten so that he dies, there shall be no
bloodguilt for him" (22:1). Or, "If a foreigner sojourns
with you in your land, you shall not do him wrong. The
foreigner who sojourns with you shall be to you like the
native born among you, and you shall love him as one of
your own; for you were foreigners in the land of Egypt.
I am the Lord your God" (Leviticus 19:33–4). In general,
Israelite civil law was expressed casuistically, and the ritual
law apodictically.

It would seem that the Israelites borrowed to some extent
from the legal codes of the Babylonians, Hurrians, and
Canaanites. This is apparent especially in the casuistic group
of laws. The apodictic group derived primarily from their
own experiences in their nomadic wanderings in Canaan
and in the wilderness of Sinai. By and large, the Israelites
made and compiled their own laws to suit their own way
of life, and what they did borrow from others they adapted
to their own needs. The result was, as a well-known scholar
recently remarked, "Hebrew legislation suited to Hebrew
needs, and under the influence of the prophets that legislation was sublimated and ethicized. Herein, as so often, the
pupil surpassed the teacher." [6]

[6] T. J. Meek, *Hebrew Origins*, rev. ed. (New York, 1950), p. 81
of the useful chapter on "The Origin of Hebrew Law."

The Philistines

About 1175 B.C. a number of Aegean peoples were driven by northern invaders from their homes on Crete and the shores of Asia Minor and took to the sea. They failed to penetrate Egypt, but they did gain a hold on the Palestinian coast. These "sea peoples," as the Egyptians called them, had a superior military and political organization. Despite their lack of numbers, they gradually got a grip on the coastal plain. Among these migrant sea peoples were the Philistines. Indeed, it is from them that the name "Palestine" derives, by way of the Latinized Greek word "Palaestina," as finally impressed on the whole region by the Roman conquerors of Judah over a thousand years later.

Their closely knit political structure, coupled with the need for mercantile expansion, brought the Philistines into the hinterland. Philistine society was divided up into five important city-states, with a "tyrant," or chieftain, at the head of each. These city-states knew how to combine for military attack. Moreover, the Philistines had a virtual monopoly on the important new metal, iron, and used it for swords, ax heads, and chariots, as well as for plough tips and sickles.

The Israelites were squarely in the path of the Philistine drive to the east. Various Israelite tribes were badly hit by the systematic depredations of the strangers from the coast. Eventually the situation reached such a pass that the tribes most seriously affected were driven to submit to a central authority. This novelty, however, was not introduced without bitter resistance from diehards who maintained an extremely literal interpretation of the meaning of the Sinaitic

Covenant. The man chosen to be "king" was Saul; the opposition to him was led by Samuel, the priestly seer.

King Saul

Speaking before the elders and assembled freemen, Samuel argued that if they elected Saul to be their king they would be flouting the primacy of God. It was not his own judgeship that he was worrying about, Samuel insisted, but the judgeship of the Lord. In addition he warned the Israelites that a king would take their sons and daughters, the best of their fields, and one-tenth of their seed and flocks. The Israelites, he said, would become the king's servants, which, in effect, meant his slaves. "And you shall cry out on that day," he said, "because of your king whom you chose for yourself, but the Lord will not answer you on that day" (I Samuel 8:18).

The Israelite assembly rejected this Catonian warning, and chose Saul, of the tribe of Benjamin, to be their first king. Saul was a striking figure, a man among men. "There was not among the Israelites a better person than he," we are told, "from his shoulders and upward he was taller than any of the people" (I Samuel 9:2). When Samuel saw that further protest was useless, he anointed Saul, and thus the kingship over Israel was sanctified.

Trials of King Saul

Almost at once Saul's royal authority was tested; shortly after assuming office, he summoned all Israel to raise the Ammonite siege of Jabesh-gilead in Transjordan. Saul threatened to destroy the herds of any able-bodied Israelite who failed to answer the call. He raised a force large enough to beat off the Ammonites, but the response of the tribes was still far from unanimous. Saul's close followers proposed that he destroy the slackers, but he refused. Again, in battle against the Philistines at Michmash, part of Saul's army deserted, and but for a clever strategem devised by Jonathan, the crown prince, the day would have been lost.

Then, after another victory, this time over the Amalekites, Saul's political star began to fade. The conservative element led by Samuel consistently undercut the king. Their support was grudging; they gave him little credit when he won and loudly condemned him when he lost. And meanwhile Saul was the prey of his own tempestuous and moody nature, which from time to time floundered in fits of envy and rage.

On one occasion Saul suddenly lost confidence in himself, when he was faced, in the Shefelah foothills near Azekah, by a Philistine army led by the giant Goliath. The once-powerful monarch was "dismayed and greatly afraid" (I Samuel 17:11). The occasion presented itself for an unknown lad, David, son of Jesse of Bethlehem, to step into the breach. Slaying the monster Goliath, he became the boy hero of all Israel. Thereafter David's rise was meteoric. He could do no wrong, fortune smiled on him at every turn. Saul made David a military chieftain and, because of his additional talents, also personal court musician, to play soothing music when "the evil spirit of God" came upon the king.

The King Comes to Grief

Saul soon realized that David was becoming the center of popular favor and was threatening to reap the political rewards of fame. "Saul has slain his thousands," the people sang, "but David—his ten thousands!" Even Jonathan, the king's son, regarded David as his bosom friend. Saul tried

several times to kill his younger rival. The jealous idea became fixed in Saul's head, the Biblical authors tell us (I Samuel 18–30), that if he could only rid himself of the upstart,
David, all would go well with him.

Saul died where he had first made his name, on the field of
battle. Against Philistines assembled in the valley of Jezreel,
Saul and his forces took up counterpositions at near-by
Mount Gilboa. In the ensuing engagement the Philistines
overwhelmed the Israelites, and Saul "took the sword and
fell upon it," rather than fall into the hands of his enemies.

Thus died Saul, the aging champion, battered to his knees,
one of the most human and touching figures in all literature.
His was a heroic and tragic role in a crucial period in Israel's
career. It was his hard lot to bear the brunt of the reaction
which is always evoked by deep social change. His own tribe
of Benjamin, while not the smallest and weakest, was not one
of the most influential. His sick nature, moreover, was a
scourge. Yet the fact remains that Saul laid the foundation
for an effective opposition to the Philistine advance, for an
attack on their valuable monopoly of iron, and, perhaps most
important, for a measurable degree of unification among the
individualistic tribes of Israel.

The Israelite Empire
under David and Solomon

ANCIENT Israel's Golden Era came during the tenth century B.C., when David and Solomon ruled Israel and Israel dominated western Asia. It was this period that the prophets had in mind, later, when they urged the restoration of a united Israel and called for vengeance on the foes about them. And it was among the descendants of David that they assumed the leader would be found who could make possible this achievement. Thus Isaiah affirmed: "And there shall come forth a shoot out of the stock of Jesse (the father of David). . . . And the spirit of the Lord shall rest upon him. . . . And it shall come to pass in that day that the root of Jesse, that stands for an ensign of the peoples, to him shall the nations seek, and his resting-place shall be glorious" (11:1–10).

Recent discoveries have greatly enhanced the historical value of the Biblical account, and even enriched its three-thousand-year-old story with considerable new material. The Queen of Sheba, after she met Solomon, is reported to have exclaimed, "It was a true report that I heard in my country concerning your achievements and your wisdom.

III. The united Israelite empire under David and Solomon (tenth century B.C.).

But I did not believe the reports until I came, and my own eyes saw. Indeed, the half of it was not told me. You have wisdom and prosperity exceeding the report that I heard" (I Kings 10:6–7). The same words might well express the mood of modern scholars rereading the Biblical history of the reigns of David and Solomon in the light of the recent revelations.

David the Favorite

David, having achieved military distinction at a very early age, began to assume the stature of a legendary figure almost before his mature life was well begun. He is credited with having killed a lion and a bear even before his dramatic conquest of the Philistine Goliath (I Samuel 16–17). Because of these precocious triumphs he won extraordinary popularity among the people.

Saul at first made David his protégé, married him to his daughter Michal, and acknowledged him favorite of the court. But David's popularity could know no bounds, and as it continued to swell among the people the king grew jealous and finally turned on him with pent-up fury. Driven from the court, David maintained his place in the hearts of the people by his gallant and resourceful acts. He sent his parents to Moab for safety, while he himself sought refuge, now at the sanctuary of Nob near Jerusalem, now at the court of Achish, the Philistine king of Gath and enemy of Saul. For a time, too, he led a band of several hundred outlaws in the Shefelah foothills in the region of Adullam. And again he proved his mettle by serving as border guard in the south for the Philistines (I Samuel 21–30). Several times during his banishment he could have killed Saul, but his deep nobility of character prevented this final desperate act.

Defeated by the Philistines at Mount Gilboa, the Israelites were left leaderless and vulnerable. By this victory the Philistines had secured the valley of Jezreel, the principal commercial and military highway from the sea into the valley of the Jordan. As a result of their defeat the Israelites seemed poised on the verge of complete disintegration, like the Canaanites before them. From this fate they were saved by David and his followers.

David Acquires the Throne of Saul

Immediately on the death of Saul, a struggle broke out for the succession to his power. Some supported Ishbosheth (Esh-baal), a son of Saul, while others, particularly the tribe of Judah, demanded David as king (II Samuel 2–4).[1] To seize and consolidate the royal power David had to resolve both domestic and foreign problems. On the one hand he had to acquire sole authority in Israel, and on the other hand he had to unite Israel and check the Philistine drive.

In the bloody battle which ensued, David and his followers left no room for doubt as to which group was to rule in Israel. To some supporters of Ishbosheth, death was meted out—not always, it appears, with David's knowledge or consent; to others, such as Mephibosheth, the crippled son of Jonathan, mercy was shown (II Samuel 9). Not relying completely on his fellow-Israelites, David hired mercenaries from Crete and elsewhere, the traditional "Cherethites and Pelethites" (II Samuel 8:18; 15:18), who served as his bodyguard.

---

[1] The role of Samuel in anointing David king even before Saul died (I Samuel 16) is quite obscure. It is sometimes no longer possible to separate and to date the various strands that came to be woven together to form the Biblical Book of Samuel.

Even more important and spectacular in this swift consolidation of power and prestige were David's military triumphs. Jerusalem, then also known as Jebus, the stronghold
of the Jebusites, fell before his attack. Then, on several
occasions, he checked the Philistines, and finally he cut them
up so badly, particularly at Gath, that they never recovered
their power to threaten Israel (II Samuel 21:15–22).[2] Having secured his western and southern flanks, David sent his
forces east across the Jordan as far as Damascus and Zobah,
and in a long series of battles he subdued some of the vigorous Aramean groups, as well as the Ammonites, Moabites,
and Edomites. He even completed the destruction, which
Saul had begun, of the elusive Amalekites in the south.

By the time David's astonishing military force had spent
itself, the Israelites were in control of territories running
from Kadesh on the Orontes river in Syria to Ezion-geber
at the head of the Gulf of Aqabah. (See Map III.) The
Mediterranean coast, except for Phoenicia and small segments of Philistia, had been made tributary, and Transjordan, as far as the Arabian desert on the east, also
acknowledged David as king. These military triumphs,
moreover, greatly furthered tribal coalescence and the composition of ancient quarrels. Already Israel was becoming
a kingdom in fact, as it had been only in title under Saul.

[2] It is interesting to note that some of these battles seem to have
been decided by a fight between one or more picked warriors of
the two sides, as in the case of David and Goliath, or the twelve-man
teams which represented the forces of David and Ishbosheth. See
Y. Yadin, *Journal of the Palestine Oriental Society*, XXI (1948),
110–116.

The Setting for International Expansion

The rise of the Israelite empire can be understood properly only in the context of the entire Near East. At the turn of the second millennium not a single state in Mesopotamia, Asia Minor, Syria, and Egypt—the aggressive forces normally active within the historic constellation of which Israel was a part—was powerful enough to interfere with David's plans for expansion. Babylonia had been in decline since the downfall of the Hammurabi dynasty in the sixteenth century B.C. The Hurrian state, in northeast Iraq, had been destroyed by Assyria in the thirteenth century. The latter, in turn (except briefly about 1100 under Tiglath-pileser I), was too weak to seek empire and adventure outside its territory until after 900 B.C. The Hittites, who had taken over northern Syria and the Hurrian state early in the fourteenth century, and whose power in the entire Near East at the time was equaled only by that of Egypt, collapsed before the onslaughts of the Aegean peoples at about 1200 B.C.

Egypt's power, too, had waned. The disintegration which had begun during the Twentieth Dynasty, especially after 1150, was not alleviated when the Amon priesthood and their wealthy associates assumed control of the land, shortly after 1100. Except for a brief period under Sheshonk I, the Biblical Shishak (about 925), Egypt was in no position to challenge anyone outside its borders until over four centuries later, when her power revived under Necho of the Twenty-sixth Dynasty. As for the Arameans (Syrians), their ascendancy in upper Transjordan, where they eventually founded a number of city-states, had only just begun.

In the context of this political void which was western

Asia about 1000 B.C., the Biblical account of the rise of David's empire bears eloquent testimony to the skillful manner in which the Israelites moved to fill the vacuum.

Israel and Phoenicia

Only against Phoenicia David did not go to battle; to do so was neither necessary nor desirable. The once-great Canaanite civilization had been reduced to a narrow coastal strip running from near modern Haifa to beyond Byblos. Here the Phoenician remnant flourished.

The Israelites under David and the Phoenicians under Hiram I entered into a mutually beneficial military and political understanding. The Phoenicians agreed to provide the Israelites with skilled engineers and craftsmen, and with cedar and cypress timber from Lebanon. As a matter of fact they built David a palace (II Samuel 5:11), for which he, in turn, probably paid more in protection and non-aggression than in silver and gold. After all, Phoenicia was militarily and economically at the mercy of Israel, and it could hope to retain its independence and increase its wealth only so long as it was useful to Israel's kings.

This situation made it possible, as well as geographically necessary, for the Phoenicians to concentrate on maritime expansion. Within a very brief period they had reached almost every part of the Mediterranean basin—Spain, Sardinia, Corsica, Sicily, and north-central Africa (later Carthage)—with their commercial undertakings, colonial activity, or cultural influence. In fact, Greece and Rome (and through them ultimately a great proportion of the entire world) acquired from the Phoenicians an alphabet in which to record the *Odyssey* and the *Iliad* and the other epics which had come into being, orally perhaps, during the era corresponding to the Biblical Period of the Judges.[3]

The New Administration

Thus within one generation the tribes of Israel came into the imperial splendor so often promised in the Pentateuch and created a national capital where none had previously existed. Shifting his headquarters from Hebron in Judah to newly conquered Jerusalem, David made this the private domain of his royal court. Existing outside all tribal jurisdiction, and belonging solely to the king, it came frequently to be called "The City of David."

The centralization of political authority in the abode of the king called for a corresponding focus for religious jurisdiction, and David's ministers began to plan the erection of a royal chapel, a magnificent edifice which would represent the earthly dwelling of Israel's invisible God. To provide fitting service for the Temple, a priesthood was established and musical guilds were organized, the latter in all likelihood by David, who was a distinguished musician and composer in his own right. Abiathar, who had assisted David at Nob, and Zadok, both of whom boasted ancient and distinguished ancestry, were appointed priests to David. Later the Zadokites, descendants real or nominal of this same Zadok, were to become the principal caste of Temple priests.

The centralization of power in David's hands was implemented further by the creation of new administrative

[3] See W. F. Albright, *American Journal of Archaeology,* LIV (1950), 162–176; D. Diringer, *The Alphabet* (New York, 1948); C. H. Gordon, *Introduction to Old Testament Times* (Ventnor, N.J., 1953), ch. vii.

and military systems. The boundaries of a number of tribes were altered on the excuse—plausible enough—of increasing fiscal and administrative efficiency, but more likely for the larger purpose of weakening tribal independence. The new units were to be represented at the court in Jerusalem, not in the traditional manner by the heads of the tribes and families, but by royal officials. And thus the way was paved for the collection of the taxes which were the price of monarchy.

The army was transformed into a permanent professional body, and the command reorganized to centralize control in Jerusalem directly under the king's authority. Abner, the commander-in-chief under Saul and Ishbosheth, was killed, and he was replaced by David's colorful nephew and devoted friend, Joab, one of the most underrated personalities in the Bible.

For the first time in Israelite history, the government introduced forced labor. Every able-bodied resident in Israel was made subject to labor service without compensation. This innovation, in turn, was probably the chief motivation behind the census which David caused to be taken throughout the land.

Imperial consolidation went on apace. Plans were projected for building the Temple and the government palaces in Jerusalem, and a pattern was determined for "the courses of the priests and the Levites and all the work of the service of the house of the Lord" (I Chronicles 28:11–19). David recognized the need for fortified sites scattered through the land and for administrative centers such as Megiddo. All of this involved a great building program, which, taken together with the development of the new army, the expansion of administrative services, the reorganization of the royal household, and the like, required unprecedented quantities of money, men, and supervision.

The supervision was provided by the newly created court bureaucracy composed of scribes, heralds, recorders, ministers, stewards, and clerks, assembled in such numbers that not all of them were Israelites. To find sufficient money and manpower it was necessary to resort to booty and tribute from conquered peoples and to taxation and *corvée* at home. This vast program set the stage for David to become the great builder and organizer, as well as the military hero of Israel.

Before he could put all these magnificent plans into action, however, David died, so that his actual building was limited to the fortification of a few key sites against the Philistines, such as Tell Beit Mirsim (perhaps Biblical Kiriat-sepher) in the southern Shefelah, Beth-shemesh in the northern Shefelah, and Tell Qasileh near the Mediterranean Sea,[4] and to the erection of royal buildings in Jerusalem and perhaps also in Megiddo.

King David, the Personality

The Biblical tradition attributes to David many qualities, but none more endearing perhaps than his gift for poetry and music. In all probability he must have composed at least some parts of the psalms which the Bible attributes to him, in addition to the famous lament over Saul and Jonathan (II Samuel 1:17–27). David's reputation was so great, how-

[4] Inside modern Tel Aviv. See B. Maisler's report on "The Excavations at Tell Qasile," *Israel Exploration Journal*, I (1950–1951), 61–76, 125–140, 194–218. See now S. Yeivin, "Social, Religious and Cultural Trends in Jerusalem under the Davidic Dynasty," *Vetus Testamentum*, III (1953), 149–166.

ever, that many psalms composed either before or after his
reign came to be associated with his name. Indeed, the official collection of the first 72 psalms—though not the entire book of 150 psalms, as popular belief has since assumed
—was attached to his name.

David's loves and hates have gripped the emotions and
imaginations of people from his day down through the ages.
Most famous of all, perhaps, was his deep affection for
Jonathan, but the mere mention of David conjures up the
names of Absalom, of Abigail, and the beautiful Bath-sheba.
In each of these stories kingly grandeur is blended with
human weakness in a way that has touched and captivated
each succeeding generation of readers.

On one of the rare occasions when a significant portion
of the population sided with an armed revolt against David's
rule, there was among the leaders David's favorite son, the
charming but vacillating Absalom. Outwitted and outfought
by David's well-trained militia, the rebels were defeated,
although not yet crushed, when the implacable Joab brought
the whole revolt to its final dénouement by killing Absalom
with his own hands. It was altogether characteristic of
David's ofttimes unpredictable mood that he did not want
any harm to come to his rebellious son and that when he
heard the tragic news, "He was much moved, and went
up to the chamber over the gate, and wept; and as he went,
thus he said, 'O my son Absalom, my son, my son Absalom!
would that I died for you, O Absalom, my son, my son!' "
(II Samuel 19:1).

On those other famous occasions when he was unable
to repress his passion for Abigail, whose husband he did
not attempt to save from death, or for Bath-sheba, whose
husband he brutally caused to be killed, David neverthe-

less was genuinely repentant for having caused the death of his rivals in love, and humbly accepted the bitter rebuke of Nathan the prophet. It would be difficult to find another such intense, compulsive, dramatic, practical, talented personality in the wide range of human history, or so simple and powerful a delineation of character in all our literature.

To the Israelites after him, David was the key figure in the Golden Era of their history, a figure beyond reproach and beyond compare. After all, it was not he but his son and successor, Solomon, who carried out his projects to their ultimate, and frequently distasteful, conclusions. David fully deserved his place of honor in his people's history but, at the same time, it was largely a matter of good fortune that his good lived after him, whereas his evil was interred with Solomon's bones.

King Solomon

When David's end drew near, there was another contest for the royal succession, just as there had been at the death of Saul. In this characteristic the history of Israel is no different from that of any other comparable kingdoms in Assyria, Babylonia, or Egypt. The penalty for coming out second best in such a power struggle, normally, was death. So it was with Adonijah, the oldest son of David, who had prior claim over his half-brother, Solomon. Adonijah, indeed, had already been proclaimed king by his followers, including the redoubtable Joab, when Solomon's backers began a counterattack. Bath-sheba, David's favorite wife and Solomon's mother, joined with the prophet Nathan to persuade the aged king to name Solomon his legal heir. Bath-sheba pointed out that if Adonijah had his way she and her son would be as good as dead.

David let himself be swayed, and gave the decisive order: "Let Zadok the priest and Nathan the prophet anoint him . . . king over Israel; and blow the trumpet, and say, 'Long live King Solomon'" (I Kings 1:34). Adonijah's followers deserted him, and Solomon later found a pretext for killing Adonijah. Other supporters of Adonijah were likewise killed or banished, until "the kingship was established firmly in the hand of Solomon" (I Kings 2:46; I Chronicles 29).

Solomon's Building Program: The Temple

Solomon inherited the task of fulfilling the plans that time and circumstances had permitted his father David only to formulate and dream about; and to this program he added plans and dreams of his own. Continuing and extending the pact with Phoenicia, Solomon imported vast amounts of timber from Lebanon and recruited large numbers of engineers, overseers, and artisans for the building of the Temple.

Solomon is best remembered by his Temple. In becoming the national shrine, as David had intended that it should, the Temple completed the process of making Jerusalem the spiritual as well as the political capital of Israel; but its cost was tremendous. To finish the magnificent edifice, Solomon was obliged to levy taxes without mercy, to force tens of thousands of his subjects to serve in labor gangs, to chop cedar and cypress in Lebanon, to raft timber from Phoenicia to Joppa, and to bear it log by log to the heights of Jerusalem.

The complex of the Temple and its associated buildings formed a magnificent architectural unit. Built by Canaanite architects, it followed the style of their native temple tradition.[5] The two free-standing columns called Jachin and Boaz (I Kings 7:21), and the three main divisions of vestibule, holy place, and holy of holies, all sprang from the Canaanite convention. Their respective Hebrew names, *ulam*, *hekhal*, and *debir*—likewise the term *bayit* (house) for the whole Temple, which was "The House of the Lord" —also appear to have been borrowed from the Canaanites.

Solomon's regime was further distinguished by the erection of government buildings, and the building or rebuilding of key fortifications. It is a frequent archaeological experience to uncover the material remains of the Solomonic (Early Iron) level of Israelite towns—for example, at Megiddo, Gezer, Tell Qasileh, Ezion-geber, Hazor, and Lachish. Like the Temple, these structures were generally Phoenician in concept and in such details as the pattern of masonry, the use of capitals (which the Greeks also borrowed from the Phoenicians a couple of centuries later), and the style of gateways. The government buildings at Megiddo, with their mammoth stables that housed some 480 of Solomon's countless horses, form a particularly noteworthy example.

Solomon the Merchant Prince: Ezion-geber

Of particular interest is the famous copper refinery and seaport at Ezion-geber, on the Gulf of Aqabah, rediscovered in the early 1930's, about a third of a mile north of the present coastline. Although the site of the port had long been sought by scholars and travelers, no one was prepared

[5] See G. E. Wright, "Solomon's Temple Resurrected," *Biblical Archaeologist*, IV (May, 1941), 17–31; and P. L. Garber, "Reconstructing Solomon's Temple," *ibid.*, XIV (February, 1951), 1–24.

for the discovery of the extraordinary structure built specifically to smelt the copper ore which was dug from the
mines of near-by Sinai and Edom. Its excavator called Ezion-
geber "the Pittsburgh of Palestine, in addition to being
its most important port," and described Solomon "as a
great copper king." Ezion-geber, like the corresponding
levels from the period of Solomon at Megiddo and Tell
Qasileh, "was planned in advance, and built with considerable architectural and engineering skill at one time as an
integral whole." [6]

Solomon's great enterprise at Ezion-geber, with its seaport and fleet of merchant ships, would seem to clarify an
intriguing Biblical problem of long standing. It has often
been asked: Did the Queen of Sheba really visit Solomon,
and if so, why should she, a woman, have made the arduous
and even dangerous trip of some 1,300 miles from her country in southwest Arabia to Jerusalem, bringing with her
gifts of fabulous worth? The Bible explains: "Now when
the Queen of Sheba heard the fame of Solomon . . . she
came to test him with hard questions . . ." (I Kings
10:1–13). This explanation is clearly diplomatic. The
"hard questions" very likely revolved about matters of the
pocketbook. Our authority on Ezion-geber points out:

Solomon's shipping line evidently made such inroads in the
lucrative caravan trade controlled by the Queen of Sheba, that
she hastened to Jerusalem with all manner of presents in order
to conclude an amicable trade agreement with him. . . . A
satisfactory commercial treaty was evidently negotiated between the two sovereigns, because we are informed that 'King

[6] From N. Glueck, *The Other Side of the Jordan* (New Haven,
1940), chs. iii, iv.

Solomon gave to the Queen of Sheba all that it pleased her to ask, besides that which he gave her according to his royal bounty' [I Kings 10:13].[7]

The commercial enterprises of Solomon, handled by "the king's merchants," extended in all directions. Thus he virtually monopolized the strategic as well as lucrative horse and chariot trade; his agents bought up the horses in Cilicia and the chariots in Egypt and sold them to the Hittites, Arameans, and other peoples of the Near East (I Kings 10:28–29).

Relations with Phoenicia

The details of the economic relations between Israel and Phoenicia (cf. I Kings 5) will probably never be wholly recovered. It may be doubted that Solomon, at least in the early part of his reign, paid much into Phoenicia's governmental coffers for the men and materials that he received from Hiram. After all, Phoenicia was at the mercy of Solomon no less than of David; it was not Phoenicia but Israel which bought horses in Cilicia. On the other hand, Solomon would have had no port, refinery, fleet, or crews at Eziongeber were it not for Phoenicia, and the latter did not make this possible out of sheer good will. The Phoenicians would have preferred to direct these projects themselves, or at least to share in the profits.

In this connection the Cabul transaction is illuminating. In return for considerable material assistance in the building of the Temple and palace complexes, Solomon offered Hiram the Galilean district of Cabul, containing twenty towns. Hiram, dissatisfied with this exchange, rejected it outright. Solomon simply took back Cabul and settled it

[7] N. Glueck, in *Biblical Archaeologist*, I (September, 1938), 14.

with Israelites (I Kings 9:10–13; II Chronicles 8:1–2), leaving with the historian, as apparently with the Phoenicians,
the feeling that Solomon could do just about as he pleased.

This relationship between Israel and Phoenicia changed
radically after the death of Solomon. Israel's united kingdom split into two, and the military balance in the Near East
changed with the rise of Shishak in Egypt and with the
growth of the rival empires of Assyria and Aram. Phoenicia
continued to grow rich in her maritime and colonial ven-
tures and ceased to grant to Israel any more concessions or
favors.

The Administration of Solomon

Solomon perfected and extended the administrative organization initiated by his father, David (I Kings 4), and
so facilitated even more the collection of taxes and the
recruitment of forced labor. At the same time, he weakened
further the tribal loyalties.

For administrative purposes Israel was divided into twelve
districts, each with its own governor. But the areas of jurisdiction, it should be noted, did not necessarily coincide
with the old tribal territories. Reuben and Gad, for instance, were merged into one district. Manasseh in Transjordan was split into two districts, and the northern part
of the Plain of Sharon was taken away from the tribe
and made a separate district. In the case of Zebulun and
Simeon, these territories had ceased to represent tribal do-
mains even before the rise of the monarchy.

Excavations indicate that some of the governors, perhaps
all, lived in palaces, to which were attached storehouses for
the grain, olive oil, and cattle collected as taxes in kind.
Each governor was required to provide food for the royal

household one month out of the year. But the district of
Judah, because it provided the principal backers and lieu-
tenants of the royal house—as well as because Jerusalem,
the capital and chief city of the nation was located within
its boundaries—occupied a specially privileged position,
directly under the king. At least two of the twelve governors were not only members of the tribe of Judah but
sons-in-law of Solomon himself.

The population of the land increased. The Bible tells how
David's census takers found "in Israel eight hundred thousand warriors that drew the sword; and the men of Judah
were five hundred thousand men" (II Samuel 24:9. I Chronicles 21:5 gives a variant total). When Solomon counted
heads to plan for his labor levies, he is reported (II Chronicles 2:16–17) to have found 153,600 aliens alone. However,
there is no way of determining whether these figures are
even approximately correct, and all estimates of Israel's
population are essentially but learned guesses.

Culture and Religion

Increased prosperity and growth had marked impact on
the culture and religion of the country. Writing, uncommon although far from unknown in the times of Moses
and the judges, spread widely in Solomon's day. Royal
secretaries recorded the affairs of state, and royal archives
are referred to repeatedly in the books of Kings and Chronicles, with some variation of the formula: "And the rest of
the acts of King So-and-So and all that he did, behold they
are inscribed in the records of the royal chronicles of Israel
and Judah." Unfortunately, however, these records have
not yet been recovered by excavators.

The royal annals, in keeping with the classical Hebrew

narrative style of such other books as Judges and Samuel, were written in a highly developed Hebrew prose. Israel's poets, moreover, stood on the same high level as her writers of prose, as can readily be seen from the few samples that have been preserved, for example: Moses' Song of Triumph at the Red Sea (Exodus 15, in part), the Blessing of Moses (Deuteronomy 33, in part), the Oracles of Balaam (Numbers 23–24), and the Song of Deborah (Judges 5).[8]

The books of the Pentateuch began to take shape from material that for centuries had been orally transmitted from generation to generation. Solomon himself was a patron of literature and the arts, and it is not accidental that his name became intimately associated with such classics as Proverbs, Canticles, and Ecclesiastes. These books crystallized in their present written form after the Babylonian Exile.

Increasing economic and political contact between the Israelites and the other peoples in the Near East led inevitably to some changes in the realm of Israelite religion. It does not appear that religious syncretism was practiced in Israel, nor that basic non-Israelite beliefs found any integral place in the worship of the Lord. Israel's God remained the unique and supreme Deity; but some ceremonial practices and even theological concepts of foreign origin were absorbed into His worship. It was during Solomon's reign that this tendency toward toleration and assimilation of alien religious ideas first increased to prominence.

Canaanite elements were responsible for the main di-

[8] Other samples of early Hebrew poetry are parts of such psalms as 29 and 68, and the Psalm of Habakkuk (Chapter 3). See in general, W. F. Albright, in *Studies in Old Testament Prophecy*, ed. H. H. Rowley (Edinburgh, 1950), pp. 1–9, with full bibliography.

vergences from the worship of the Lord. Economic and political co-operation between Israel and Phoenicia led to the free exchange of cultural and religious practices as well. The worship of Baal and other prominent Phoenician deities, including some of their orgiastic elements, spread in Israel. Intermarriage with Phoenician and other non-Israelite peoples also became less rare. The king himself "loved many foreign women, besides the daughter of Pharaoh, women of the Moabites, Ammonites, Edomites, Sidonians, and Hittites" (I Kings 11:1 ff.). It is true that Solomon's acquisition of many of the alleged total of "seven hundred princesses and three hundred concubines" was motivated, as royal marriages so frequently are, by the dictates of diplomacy. But these casual marriages with foreigners brought in their wake additional concessions to alien gods. The Biblical writers did not overlook the fact that Solomon built idolatrous shrines for Ashtoreth, Milcom, Chemosh, Molech, Asherah, and other deities of the foreign princesses, just as he permitted Phoenician novelties to intrude among various aspects of the Temple cult and paraphernalia.

Tens of thousands of Israelites of the border regions of Dan, Asher, Zebulun, Naphtali, and Manasseh mingled busily with the Phoenicians. Also in commercial towns such as Tell Qasileh and border towns such as Beth-shemesh, Israelites and non-Israelites freely mixed. Small wonder that the Biblical historians of the Book of Kings blamed Solomon for this apostasy from the Lord, which, in their opinion, accounted largely for the disruption of the kingdom and the other disasters which followed his death (I Kings 11:9–13).

The Last Days of the United Kingdom

The opulence and power of Solomon's kingdom was doomed to deteriorate. Under the increasing pressure of this decline, tensions, both foreign and domestic, produced a split between politically favored Judah in the south and the northern districts which came to call themselves Israel —with "Israel" here representing a political and not a spiritual unit. It was during Solomon's reign, for example, that the regime of Pharaoh Shishak I began to restore to Egypt, if only temporarily, some of its former imperial pre-eminence. Shishak gave political refuge to rebels, both Israelite and non-Israelite, who quarreled with the royal house in Jerusalem—for example, to Jeroboam of the tribe of Ephraim and to Hadad of the royal house of Edom (I Kings 11:14 ff.). The kingdom of Aram too, under Rezon in Damascus, was becoming powerful enough to be "an adversary to Solomon all the days of his life" (I Kings 11:23–25).

In Israel, Solomon's rule brought great prosperity and prestige to the land as a whole, but it was only in a limited degree that the common people shared with the aristocracy in this new wealth and status. Forced labor, high taxes, and political corruption bred a host of enemies for the king's regime, particularly among the heavily burdened lower classes.

These grievances further aggravated the ancient distrust and resentment of the northern tribes for the Judeans and their assumed superiority. Even before Solomon's reign had drawn to its close, the situation had become critical. When Rehoboam, Solomon's son and successor, sent his tax collector, Adoniram, to treat with the Israelites under Jeroboam, he was confronted with open revolt. Adoniram was stoned to death, and Rehoboam himself barely escaped with his life (I Kings 12; II Chronicles 10). This act of violence ushered in the Divided Kingdom.

The rebel leaders of northern Israel did not oppose a monarchy, nor did they care about the kind of worship that went on in the Temple and the shrines. They were willing to support one of their own as king, in the hope and belief that this would lighten the heavy burden of taxation and increase their share in the common wealth. But the lower classes who made up the backbone of the rebellion in the North had yet to learn that what Jeroboam and the other northern leaders intended was nothing more than replacing the Judean monarchy of Solomon with another equally harsh monarchy of their own.

The Biblical historian makes it clear that if the ruling group behind Rehoboam had been willing to share the considerable wealth of the kingdom with the leading supporters of Jeroboam, the kingdom of Solomon would have endured (I Kings 12:1–19). Whether there simply was not enough wealth to satisfy both groups, or whether Rehoboam overestimated his strength, the fact remains that the North broke forever with the South.

The Divided Kingdom:
Israel and Judah

ISRAELITE civilization was not destined to make any important contributions to mankind's material progress. The physical and economic geography of the land constituted a formidable obstacle to any such achievement. The natural resources of the region lying between Dan and Beersheba were few, its population small, and economic surpluses, therefore, negligible. Unlike the Egyptians, Phoenicians, and such peoples of western Asia as the Sumerians, Babylonians, and Assyrians, the Israelites never won a major place among the great builders, merchants, or warriors of the ancient Near East.

Israel's defensive situation was not more fortunate. Having made their home in a buffer area amid stronger civilizations, the Israelites were under almost constant pressure or attack from neighbors striving, if not to conquer them outright, at least to use their land as a highway or base for invasion of some rival. Once David's reign was over, the momentary lull in the imperial struggles of western Asia came to an end. Without such a lull the Israelite empire

IV. The Divided Kingdom: Israel and Judah (ninth and eighth centuries B.C.).

could hardly have emerged at all; and when it was over, Judah and Israel had no rest. Actual invasions were not uncommon, and the threat of possible or impending attack was almost constant. These same conditions, on the other hand, provided the setting for the Israelite genius which came to express itself in the realm of culture and religion; and it was largely during the period of the Divided Kingdom that the Israelite civilization took on its definite shape and character.

The Two Kingdoms in Equilibrium

The split between Judah and Israel, following the revolt of Jeroboam, leader of the northern rebels, against Rehoboam, successor to Solomon, resulted in a stalemate. Israel, the northern segment, being larger both in total arable land and population, was wealthier than its rival. But if Judah, from whose soil the state of David had sprung, was smaller and geographically more concentrated, it was for that very reason, at least in part, more efficiently administered and far less torn by regional conflicts. Israel was united chiefly by its opposition to Judah. Several powerful groups sought the control of the country, and Jeroboam held the discordant segments of the newborn kingdom together largely because its independent existence was threatened by Rehoboam and by Abijah (Abijam), his son and successor.

Had the two kingdoms been left to themselves, either might have gained the ascendancy over its opponent. But the major factors in preserving an equilibrium were external. Egypt, for a short time, and then Aram and Assyria, managed to preserve a balance of power between the two.

The International Setting: Egypt, Aram, Assyria

After lying dormant several centuries, Egypt began to show renewed signs of imperial vigor under Shishak, founder of the Twenty-second Dynasty. By harboring such enemies of Solomon as Jeroboam and Hadad the Edomite, Shishak had helped split united Israel and then, exploiting the break, he moved at once to invade the southern kingdom of Judah.

Anticipating an Egyptian invasion, Rehoboam shelved the idea of challenging the secessionist government of Israel and instead made a feverish attempt to strengthen his own defenses (II Chronicles 11:5–12). These efforts proved of no avail when Shishak's army began to march (about 920 B.C.), and the fortified cities of Judah fell one after another until Jerusalem itself was taken and the Temple treasures sacked.

At first, northern Israel welcomed the breathing spell provided by Egypt's invasion of Judah. But Shishak's mixed hordes did not stop at the boundaries of Judah; they pushed on into the territory of Israel, as well as south into Edom and west into Philistia. Difficulties at home, however, prevented Shishak from exploiting this brilliant beginning; and except for an unsuccessful attack against Rehoboam's grandson Asa, at Mareshah, Egypt did not again disturb western Asia seriously for several centuries. Yet in one respect, at least, this isolated imperialist irruption was of great significance: it left Judah unable to re-establish its old predominance over Israel.

The split between Israel and Judah considerably hastened the emergence of several Aramean states in the northern part of the area that lay between Israel and the Euphrates, i.e., Syria. The two most prominent of these were Aram Zobah and Aram Damascus. The former controlled the area which lay east of Damascus and Hamath, and the latter, as the name would indicate, revolved essentially about the commercially important city of Damascus.

The powerful state of David and Solomon had held the various Aramean states in check. Divided, Israel and Judah were less successful. Now and then they joined forces against the Arameans, and at other times one or the other entered into a coalition with an Aramean state against her sister state. When Israel under King Baasha overran the northern part of Judah, the latter paid Ben-hadad of Aram to invade Israel and thus draw off her troops. A few decades later, however, King Jehoshaphat of Judah and King Ahab of Israel once more joined forces against Aram.

Phoenicia, too, failed to maintain its independence. Faced by the growing power first of the Arameans and later of the Assyrians, the Phoenicians continued to cultivate their neighborly relations with Israel. This policy led, among other things, to the marriage of Ahab, son of King Omri of Israel, to Jezebel, daughter of King Ittobaal of Phoenicia. Early in the ninth century, the Assyrian Ashurnasirpal II (about 883–859) managed to reduce parts of Phoenicia to a tributary status and at the same time to establish the reputation of the Assyrian armies for merciless brutality. Ashurnasirpal himself boasted over his vanquished foes, "With their blood I dyed the mountain red like wool." Under Shalmaneser III (858–824) Assyria continued its drive westward with ever-increasing military and economic pressure.

The Assyrian menace provoked a reaction in the form of a defensive coalition in the region headed by the Israelites and Arameans. The royal Assyrian chronicle recounts that King Ahab of Israel contributed 2,000 chariots and 10,000 foot soldiers to the coalition; but, in spite of this magnificence, its forces were defeated at the battle of Karkar, near Hamath (about 853). It does not appear that the Assyrian army was able to exploit the victory at once; but within ten years Shalmaneser's government was collecting tribute from states as far west as Israel and Phoenicia. From then until the Medes and a resurgent Babylonia brought her to heel some two and a half centuries later, Assyria held not only Judah and Israel but all of western Asia in her sway.

The Northern Kingdom of Israel

No single major group within Israel ever managed to dominate the entire kingdom for more than a generation or two at a time. Chronic plotting for the succession repeatedly brought kings and would-be kings to bloody ends. The dynasty of Jeroboam ended abruptly with the murder of his son Nadab. After ruling only two years, he was murdered while battling to take Gibbethon from the Philistines (about 905). His assassin, Baasha of the tribe of Issachar, seized the throne; but Baasha's son and successor, Elah, was in his turn assassinated after a reign of two years. Again the murderer, this time a certain Zimri, "commander of one-half of the chariotry," succeeded his victim, but for only seven days! To avoid the humiliation of being killed by Omri, commander-in-chief of Elah's forces, Zimri set fire to his headquarters in Tirzah and died in the holocaust.

During the next several years civil war raged in Israel between forces led by Omri and the followers of his rival,

Tibni. About 878 Omri finally gained the upper hand and established what the Assyrian royal chronicles called the "House of Omri" (I Kings 15:9 ff.; 16:1–23).

The Omride Dynasty

It was under Omri that the northern kingdom acquired, for the first time, a permanent and impressive capital. Abandoning Tirzah, which had served as a kind of capital for about forty years, Omri built a new political center, which he named Samaria. From the excavations at this site,[1] a good picture is gained of the magnificent palace and fortifications which he and his son Ahab erected there.

The house of Omri brought prosperity to the northern kingdom. Aram for the time being had ceased to threaten, Moab in Transjordan was under control, and relations with rapidly expanding Phoenicia developed along lines of mutual economic interest. This prosperity, however, was restricted almost exclusively to Israel's upper class. The common people, those who worked with their hands in the towns and on the land, derived little enough from this increasing wealth. The petty farmer frequently lost his crops and his land to the big landowner. The apprentices and artisans found the economic and social gap widening between themselves and their masters. The merchant class became richer and more influential than before. Freemen were becoming slaves, and the poor were being compelled to sell their children into bondage. Where members of the lower classes were able to obtain loans from the rich, it was usually at exorbitant rates of interest. Nor was the eco-

[1] See "Luxurious Samaria," ch. xiii in C. C. McCown, *The Ladder of Progress in Palestine* (New York, 1943), pp. 192–204.

nomic and social structure helped by the periodic droughts which came upon the land, such as the drought and famine recorded in the days of Ahab.

Ahab, Naboth, and Elijah

It was during this period that the event occurred which is recorded in I Kings 21, and is now celebrated in the annals of justice and literature. Naboth, a commoner, owned a vineyard which lay next to King Ahab's palace. The king, determined to acquire the land for a vegetable garden, made the owner several offers for his vineyard. But Naboth, a man of strong ancestral sentiment, would not trade or sell the property he had inherited from his fathers. Thereupon Jezebel, Ahab's Phoenician wife, took matters into her own hands. She bribed two men to accuse Naboth falsely of having committed blasphemy to God and treason to the king. Naboth and his heirs were stoned to death, and the king got his vineyard.

At this juncture the prophet Elijah stepped forth and denounced the injustice of the royal couple in blunt terms: "Have you murdered, and you will take possession too?" And he went on to curse the king, saying, "So said the Lord, 'In the place where the dogs licked the blood of Naboth, shall the dogs lick your blood, even you'" (I Kings 21:19).

Elijah was acting in the prophetic tradition of righteousness. His act recalls that of the prophet Nathan in the previous century, who, in the memorable parable of the lone lamb which the rich man took from his poor neighbor, fearlessly condemned David for causing the death of Uriah, the husband of Bath-sheba (II Samuel 11–12).

A combination of external and domestic developments ended the Omride dynasty when King Joram (or Jehoram), younger son of Ahab, was killed. On the death of Ahab, King Mesha of Moab rose up to shake off the Israelite yoke.[2] In the face of this new threat, Judah and Edom allied themselves with Israel and went forth in battle against Moab. The campaign was only partially successful (II Kings 3).

Aram, in the meantime, took advantage of the turmoil to make several raids on Israel, even besieging Samaria, the capital city. During one of the battles against the Arameans in Transjordan, King Joram of Israel was wounded. While recuperating in Jezreel, he was attacked and killed by a mutinous section of his own army. The leader of the revolt, Jehu, then seized the throne (about 842).

The Dynasty of Jehu

The new monarch initiated a sweeping purge of the Omride household and its chief supporters. He killed Jezebel and all of Ahab's heirs and "all who remained of the house of Ahab in Jezreel, and all his great men, and his intimate friends, and his priests, until he left him no remnant" (II Kings 10:11).

Aram continued to be a constant threat during the Jehu dynasty. When King Hazael threatened Israel, Jehu paid tribute to Shalmaneser of Assyria to keep the Syrian ruler in check. This event has become famous because Shalmaneser's Black Obelisk, discovered in his palace in 1846, records and illustrates the transaction. The bas-relief clearly pictures the Israelite delegation, headed by a prostrate figure—either Jehu or his personal deputy—bringing the tribute to "the mighty monarch." [3]

[2] See "The Moabite Stone" in J. Finegan, *Light from the Ancient Past* (Princeton, 1946), pp. 157–158.

[3] *Ibid.*, pp. 172–173 and Fig. 73.

Later, when the Assyrians developed troubles of their own at home, their domination of Israel was replaced by that of the Arameans, under Hazael and his son Ben-hadad. But Aram, in its turn, was rent and weakened by civil war, thus giving the kingdom of Israel the opportunity to embark once again on an extended period of expansion and prosperity.

The long reign of Jeroboam II witnessed the spectacular, if only temporary, reconquest of a considerable part of the area originally controlled by David and Solomon. The territory across the Jordan which had been lost to Aram was recovered. The Bible records that Jeroboam "restored the boundary of Israel from the entrance of Hamath as far as the Sea of the Arabah" (II Kings 14:25). None of Assyria, Aram, or Judah was in a position to interfere with Israel's limited objectives, and the Phoenicians profited with Israel through their long-established policy of co-operation. Excavations of such cities as Samaria and Megiddo have uncovered striking evidence of Israel's increased wealth during this period. It seemed that northern Israel was once again well on the way to prosperity and peace.

Amos and Hosea

Once again, however, royal arrogance and preoccupation with narrowly selfish aims provoked a ringing challenge. As Nathan had confronted David, as Elijah had berated Ahab and Jezebel, now Amos spoke out, even at the temple of Bethel in Israel. As a herdsman of Tekoa in Judah, Amos saw a most gloomy picture within the gilded frame of royal riches. As fast as the upper classes were acquiring wealth, the poorer groups were sinking into a disastrous economic and social decline. He realized that on such a foundation the stability of Israel could not endure.

In tirades which have never been equaled in their majestic force or terrible beauty, Amos denounced King Jeroboam II. Like Elijah and Elisha before him, like Deborah, Samuel, and Nathan before them, Amos saw in his God the complete sovereign not only of His own chosen land and people but of the peoples and lands which surrounded Israel as well. The king and his supporters, Amos warned, had broken the Covenant with God: "They sold the righteous for money, and the needy for the price of a pair of sandals." In the name of God, Amos portrayed with thunderous phrase the mortal peril of a society in which the powerful "trample the head of the poor into the dust of the earth, and turn aside the way of the humble . . . so that they have profaned My holy name" (Amos 2:6–7).

The same dire warning was hurled at Israel by the prophet Hosea, an Israelite contemporary of Amos. Knowing intimately all phases of her life, Hosea dwelt upon Israel's faithless desertion of the Lord for the gods of the Phoenicians and the idols of the heathen. Her leaders and priests, even her prophets, he charged, shared in the common acts of sin and sacrilege. Thus to depend on fortified cities, on impotent idols, and on Assyrian might, he warned Israel, was to invite disaster and exile. Only if Israel turned back to God, could the catastrophe be averted:

> Samaria shall bear her guilt,
>> Because she had rebelled against her God.
> They shall fall by the sword,
>> Their infants shall be dashed in pieces,
>> And their pregnant women ripped open.

Return, O Israel, to the Lord your God,
For you have stumbled in your iniquity
[Hosea 14: 1–2; 13: 16 f. in English versions].

The warnings of Amos and Hosea were fulfilled. The dynasty of Jehu, like that of Omri, came to a catastrophic end. After a rule of six months, Zachariah, son of Jeroboam, was assassinated by the adventurer Shallum, who himself was cut down a short month later by a certain Menahem of Tirzah (about 750).

The Fall of Israel

By this time, in truth, it made very little difference who ruled Israel, for Assyria once again had begun its massive westward thrust in the greatest phase of its imperialist expansion. Tiglath-pileser III conquered all of western Asia and carried off to distant lands large segments of the conquered populations.

Menahem prevented the total devastation of the country only by paying heavy tribute, which he raised with a crushing levy on the people. Their plight can be read in the Assyrian annals in which Tiglath-pileser is made to boast:

As for Menahem, I overwhelmed him [like a snowstorm] and he . . . fled like a bird alone. . . . I returned him to his place [and imposed tribute upon him]. . . . Israel [literally "Omri-Land"] . . . all its inhabitants [and] their possessions I led to Assyria. They overthrew their King Pekah and I placed Hoshea as king over them. I received from them 10 talents of gold, 1,000 [?] talents of silver as their tribute and brought them to Assyria.[4]

[4] A. Leo Oppenheim, in *Ancient Near Eastern Texts,* ed. J. B. Pritchard (Princeton, 1950), pp. 283–284.

The Pekah referred to in the Assyrian inscription was a military commander who had killed Menahem's son, Pekahiah, and then usurped his throne. Pekah made common cause with King Rezin of Aram against Judah. The allies advanced well into Judean territory before they were thwarted by a mercenary Assyrian army hastily summoned by King Ahaz of Judah. And soon after this check, Pekah lost both his life and throne to a rival called Hoshea.

The new Israelite administration, not being content to remain a mere vassal of Assyria, withheld tribute on several occasions and began negotiations for a coalition with Egypt. Thus flouted, the Assyrians decided to put a stop, once and for all, to the spirit of resistance and intrigue which still smoldered in Israel.

The Assyrian army under Shalmaneser V marched into Israel and for three years besieged the capital Samaria. Not until Shalmaneser was succeeded by his commander-in-chief, Sargon II, did the Assyrians smash through the crumbling defenses and put the city to fire and sword. Thus the sovereignty of the northern kingdom of Israel came to a final end (about 722).

Sargon always took great pride in his capture of Samaria. He records in his Annals:

At the beginning of my royal rule, I besieged and conquered Samaria, led away as booty 27,290 inhabitants of it. I formed from them a contingent of 50 chariots and made the remaining [inhabitants] assume their [social] positions. I installed over them an officer of mine and imposed upon them the tribute of the former king.[5]

[5] From the Annals of Sargon II, in Oppenheim, *op. cit.*, pp. 284–285; cf. Finegan, *op. cit.*, pp. 173–176.

This depletion of Israel by forced exile had its counter-part in the resettlement throughout the land of Canaan of Babylonians, Elamites, Arameans, and others drawn from other conquered territories. This deportation has given rise to a double misconception: first, that there were ten tribes in northern Israel at the time of its destruction, and secondly, that these ten tribes were "lost," only to reappear elsewhere in the world. Time and again, peoples the world over have claimed descent from these "Ten Lost Tribes."

There were not, in fact, ten distinct tribes in Israel at the time of Sargon the Assyrian; and the exiles were lost only in the sense that they were absorbed wherever they were transplanted.[6] Probably only a few of the descend-ants of the Israelite exiles remained true to the God and land of Israel and managed, nearly a century and a half later, to join with the exiles of Judah.

The foreigners who were thus introduced into Israel also tended to lose their cultural identity in a general amalgama-tion. It was this resettlement, with its inevitable effect on religious and social customs, which set the stage for the rise of the anti-Judean group among the Samaritans that resisted the restoration of Jerusalem and the Temple later on when the Persians had come to power.

The Southern Kingdom of Judah

The history of Judah generally paralleled that of Israel, with the one qualification that Judah tended to be weak when Israel was strong, and prospered when Israel was weak. For one thing, the area from Dan to Beersheba, with its limited natural resources and economic advantages, did

[6] See the discussion by H. G. May, *Biblical Archaeologist,* VI (Sept., 1943), 55-60.

not seem able to support two prosperous kingdoms at once. Agriculture, commerce, the handicrafts, and the tribute of weaker nations formed the major sources of income of both countries. Another important factor in this relationship was the intervention of neighboring powers—whether Assyria, the Aramean states, Phoenicia, Egypt, or the Transjordan countries—that tended to keep the two divided and unequal. Only occasionally did circumstances combine to allow an effective and equal alliance between Israel and Judah.

Finally, there was one more difference: Judah lasted longer. The southern kingdom, consisting of only two tribes, Judah and Benjamin, both of which remained loyal to the line and tradition of David, was far more compact and therefore capable of reacting with much greater coherence and agility. Then, too, Judah did not lie directly across the path of conquerors and was much less a prize than Israel, besides being less important as an ally or a potential foe to either Assyria or Aram.

Under Asa and Jehoshaphat

During most of the long reigns of Asa and his son Jehoshaphat (about 912–849), Judah and the dynasty of David continued to prosper. Asa's administration stabilized the position of the land. Asa checked the Egyptian army under Zerah the Ethiopian at Mareshah (II Chronicles 14:8–14) and bribed Ben-hadad of Aram to attack Baasha of Israel, to force Baasha to raise his siege of northern Judah.

He also carried out a program of religious reform. Early in his career he abolished male prostitution and various forms of idolatry, alien elements which had no rightful place alongside the worship of the Lord. In all of this he had the vigorous encouragement of the prophet Azariah. Later, however, the seer Hanani accused Asa of basing his policy on the favor of Ben-hadad of Aram rather than on fear of the Lord (I Kings 15; II Chronicles 15–16). For this attack, the king had the seer imprisoned; but the precise social circumstances surrounding these actions can no longer be determined.

Faced by the growing menace of the Arameans and Assyrians, Jehoshaphat then concluded a pact with Israel, and his son Joram (or Jehoram) was married to Athaliah, daughter of Ahab and Jezebel. But not all the Judeans favored the alliance of the government with that of Ahab. Indeed, on one occasion when Jehoshaphat returned from an ill-starred joint military venture with Israel against Ramoth-gilead in Transjordan, then in Aramean hands, Jehu, son of Hanani the seer denounced him: "Should you help the wicked, and love those who hate the Lord?" (I Kings 22; II Chronicles 18; 19:2).

The Judean government levied tribute on the Philistines and Arabs, garrisoned the fortified cities of the land, and defeated a coalition of Ammonites, Moabites, and Edomites. For a time Judah held sway over the southern part of Transjordan all the way to Ezion-geber. Jehoshaphat rebuilt the harbor there and in a joint venture with Ahab's older son Ahaziah launched a new merchant fleet. The prophet Eliezer protested vehemently against this act of co-operation with Israel. In any case, the ships were wrecked, and the project was not repeated. But in another joint venture with Israel, that of collecting tribute from the Moabites, Jehoshaphat was somewhat more successful.

Judicial Reforms

An important development in this period was the reorganization of the Judean judicial system. The authority of the "elders" and the "heads of the tribes" had been on the wane ever since the days of the United Kingdom. The Bible reports that David and Solomon themselves acted as judges (II Samuel 15:2–6; I Kings 3:9–12) and appointed judges who, like the district governors, were responsible directly to them. Even the priests and Levites who administered the religious law and formed a kind of civil service were personally responsible to the king.

Probably because the civil administration of justice had become corrupt (cf. II Chronicles 19:6–7), Jehoshaphat cleaned out the old system and appointed Levites, priests, and prominent laymen to administer both the religious and civil law. The Bible says of this reform:

And, behold, Amariah the chief priest shall be over you in all [religious] matters of the Lord, and Zebadiah the son of Ishmael, the leader of the house of Judah, shall be over you in all the king's [civil] matters; and the officers of the Levites shall be before you. Deal courageously, and may the Lord be with the good! [verse 11].[7]

In all likelihood, the religious and civil spheres of the law were frequently too closely intertwined to be administered separately by religious and lay officials. In any case, it would appear that the judicial reforms of Jehoshaphat made it easier for the high priest to replace the king as the chief

[7] See the discussion by W. F. Albright, in the *Alexander Marx Jubilee Volume*, ed. S. Lieberman (New York, 1950), pp. 61–82.

judge of the land after the return from the Babylonian Exile.

Conflict and Instability

During the eight-year reign of Jehoshaphat's son, Joram (or Jehoram), and during the brief reigns of Joram's successors, Ahaziah his son, and Athaliah his wife, Judah's position deteriorated steadily. Internal instability was reflected in Joram's murder of his six brothers, to whom "their father had given great gifts, of silver, and of gold, and of precious things, with fortified cities in Judah" (II Chronicles 21:1ff.). Also during this period the Edomites revolted from Judah, achieving a measure of independence; and Philistine and Arabian marauders invaded the royal palace and made off with its treasures, the royal wives, and all the princes but one.

Ahaziah, the lone survivor, had reigned but one year when he was killed during a visit to his uncle, King Joram of Israel. His mother Athaliah proceeded to murder all but one of her grandsons and to usurp the throne. Thus a full-blooded Phoenician woman, Jezebel, was the power behind the throne of Ahab in Israel, and her half-Phoenician daughter was on the throne in Judah. Athaliah was deposed and killed six years later, and Joash (or Jehoash), the single grandson who had escaped her murderous net, assumed the kingship about 836.

Under Joash and his son Amaziah, Judah's troubles continued. Joash was defeated by Hazael of Aram, and Amaziah's conquest of Edom was nullified by a disastrous defeat at the hands of King Joash of Israel. Amaziah, like his father Joash before him, was murdered by a rival group, but the murder of Amaziah occurred twelve years after he had been dethroned in favor of his son Uzziah (or Azariah) (II Kings 14; II Chronicles 25).[8]

Under Uzziah

During the long reign of Uzziah and the shorter one of his son and coregent Jotham (about 775–735), Judah reached the peak of its power and prosperity. Free of any threat of interference by Israel, Uzziah was able to effect impressive improvements in his people's position both at home and abroad. The army was enlarged, reorganized, and supplied with the latest weapons and engines of siege. Key sites were fortified. Recalcitrant Philistine cities, such as Gath, Jabneh, and Ashdod, were reduced to subjection. The Ammonites and other peoples of Transjordan were conquered and laid under tribute. In the Negeb, all the way to Ezion-geber and even beyond into Arabia, agriculture, commerce, and building flourished as never before (II Chronicles 26).

Assyrian Domination of Judah: Isaiah

Under Tiglath-pileser III Assyria was on the march again. Judah formed a defensive coalition with Israel, Aram, and other nations against the Mesopotamian menace; but it was

[8] It is interesting to note that after the United Kingdom split into two, the kingdom of Judah, unlike that of Israel, continued to share with the other Near Eastern countries the use of the throne name in place of the private name. Thus Solomon had a second name, Jedidiah, though it is not certain which was the private name originally (II Samuel 12:24–25). Uzziah replaced the private name Azariah, etc. See the discussion by A. M. Honeyman in *Journal of Biblical Literature*, LXVII (1948), 13–25. Names such as Joash and Joram, however, are only abbreviated forms of Jehoash and Jehoram, and have no honorific significance.

with the greatest difficulty that the little kingdom, now ruled by Jotham's son Ahaz, retained some semblance of her former independence.

On two occasions Judah was able to save her territory and her population, if not her dignity and sovereignty, by submitting to Assyria, once when King Rezin of Aram and King Pekah of Israel made a joint attack against her (about 735), and again, about a decade later, during Israel's fatal revolt against Assyria.

On the first occasion Ahaz purchased Tiglath-pileser's assistance in driving off the two invaders. And again a prophet, this time Isaiah, warned Ahaz that Judah would become the arena for a struggle between the major powers. In vivid language Isaiah exhorted the king: "Take heed and be calm; fear not, and let not your heart be faint because of these two tails of smoking firebrands"—as he scornfully called Rezin and Pekah—and assured him that within a few years "the land before whose two kings you are in dread will be forsaken" (Isaiah 7). Relentlessly the prophet continued to warn that, if Ahaz stubbornly refused to heed the word of the Lord, "Then it shall come to pass in that day that every place where there were a thousand vines worth a thousand pieces of silver will become briers and thorns. . . . It shall become a place where oxen are sent forth and where sheep tread" (Isaiah 7:23–25).

Judah's tribute to Assyria must have been considerable, yet on the surface her prosperity appeared to continue. This impression may have been due, in part at least, to the fact that her surrounding rivals had likewise been weakened by Assyria.

Under Hezekiah and Manasseh: Micah

After Israel's fall, Merodach-baladan, king of Babylon, tried to form a coalition with Judah and organize western Asia to defy Assyria. And again Isaiah came forth and warned Hezekiah, son of Ahaz, that he would be trapped in the middle of a bitter struggle. The prophet thundered:

Hear the word of the Lord. Behold, the days are coming when all that is in your house, and that which your fathers treasured up until this day, will be carried off to Babylon. . . . And some of your sons who are born to you shall be taken captive, and they shall be eunuchs in the palace of the king of Babylon. [II Kings 20:16–18; Isaiah 39:6–7].

Isaiah was joined by another prophet, Micah, native of Moresheth, near Philistine Gath in the Shefelah. In the spirit of Hosea before him, who had described Israel as "mixing herself among the nations . . . like a silly dove, without understanding" (Hosea 7:8–11), Micah had already excoriated Israel for her reliance on the power of foreign allies instead of on the strength of the Lord. Now in His name he warned the people again:

I will make of Samaria heaps in the field,
   A place for planting vineyards,
And I will pour down her stones into the valley,
   And her foundations I will uncover [Micah 1:6].

Moreover, he continued, Israel's doom would extend to Judah, for Judah was guilty of the same sins:

The godly man has perished from the land,
   And the upright among men is no more.
They all lie in wait for blood,
   And each stalks his brother with a net [Micah 7:2].

Judah's leaders, her prophets, her judges, her priests, and her rich men were all misleading her. Trusting in burnt offerings and empty sacrifices, they ignored Micah's classic injunction:

> Only to do justice
> and to love loyally
> and to walk humbly with your God [6:8].

The ominous warnings of Isaiah and Micah went unheeded. Shortly after 715, Assyria invaded the rebellious states and crushed them. Another major invasion took place about 701. The Assyrian forces under Sennacherib subjugated most of western Asia, and the enemy threatened Jerusalem itself. Interestingly, the Biblical account of this event (II Kings 18–19; Isaiah 36–38) is supplemented by the Assyrian chronicle. Together they paint a vivid picture of the campaign. Sennacherib, in his chronicle, boasts:

As for Hezekiah the Judean, he did not submit to my yoke, I laid siege to 46 of his strong cities, walled forts, and to the countless small villages in their vicinity, and conquered them . . . I drove out of them 200,150 people . . . [Hezekiah] himself I made a prisoner in Jerusalem, his royal residence, like a bird in a cage.[9]

The Assyrian army, however, did not take Jerusalem. A plague, achieving what the Judeans could not, laid the invaders low and spared the city. As the story is told by the Biblical chronicler: "That night the angel of the Lord went forth and struck 185,000 in the camp of Assyria. And when men arose early in the morning, behold, they were all dead corpses. And Sennacherib king of Assyria departed,

[9] After Oppenheim, *op. cit.*, p. 288.

and went and returned, and dwelt at Nineveh" (II Kings 19:35–36).

During the reign of Hezekiah, a great engineering feat was accomplished. Lacking an adequate supply of water, Jerusalem was dangerously vulnerable to siege. To obviate this fatal weakness, workmen using hand tools cut a tunnel about six feet high through more than half a mile of solid rock. Starting from the two ends, the workmen met at about the middle, a remarkable feat to be performed without benefit of surveyor's instruments. Thus the pool of Siloam inside the city was connected directly with the Gihon spring outside, and the achievement was commemorated by the so-called "Siloam Inscription" which was carved in the solid rock.[10]

Hezekiah's administration also put through several religious reforms (II Chronicles 29–30). The Temple and its paraphernalia were purified, the priestly and Levitic orders were reorganized, idolatrous objects and sites throughout the land were destroyed, and the celebration of the passover, long neglected by many, was once more generally revived. This revival was seized upon as an occasion to urge the Israelite population to make the pilgrimage to Jerusalem for the celebration of the feast and the renewal of their membership in the Judean kingdom. It is recorded, however, that "when the [Judean] couriers passed from city to city through the country of Ephraim and Manasseh and as far as Zebulun, they laughed them to scorn, and mocked them" (30:10).

The long reign of Hezekiah's son, Manasseh, traditionally fifty-five years and the longest in the history of Judah or

[10] See "The Siloam Tunnel," in Finegan, *op. cit.*, pp. 158–160, and Figs. 68–69.

Israel, was remembered by the Biblical writer for "the evil that he did in the eyes of the Lord" (II Kings 21:2). He reintroduced the idolatrous objects and shrines which his father had removed, and "shed . . . much innocent blood, until he had filled Jerusalem from one end to another." But it must be borne in mind that during this period Judah was a vassal of the renowned Assyrians, Esarhaddon and Ashurbanipal (about 681–630).[11]

Josiah and the Reformation: Jeremiah

Amon, son of the long-lived Manasseh, had been on the throne only two years when he was murdered in a palace revolution. The conspirators, probably an anti-Assyrian group, were in turn killed by another group, known as "the people of the land," who then proceeded to proclaim Amon's son, Josiah, as king. These events occurred about 640, in the midst of the period of Assyrian domination.

Possibly with the full knowledge of Assyria, Josiah began to act with a remarkable show of independence; he seems even to have entertained hopes of taking over Israel, now an Assyrian colony. The Judean government was able to reorganize and enlarge the army, as well as to nurture other bold designs, because Assyria was being challenged by powerful peoples round about her in Mesopotamia.

About 621, while catastrophe was brewing for Assyria, and unbeknownst to anyone, for Judah as well, Josiah effected the sweeping religious reforms subsequently known

[11] The author of II Chronicles 33 tells us that the Lord punished Manasseh for his wickedness by causing him to be taken captive to Babylon, and that when the king repented of his sins, the Lord caused him to be restored to his throne in Jerusalem, from where he instituted sweeping religious reforms. The true historical picture is not clear.

as the Reformation of Josiah. Unlike so many of its predecessors, Josiah's regime was not content merely to cleanse the Temple of idolatrous objects and rites and to reorganize its services and priesthood. Rounding up the priests who had abetted alien practices, Josiah had them slain, and at the same time he abolished all shrines except the Temple in Jerusalem. He incorporated the dislodged priests in the purged guild at Jerusalem (II Kings 22–23).

The religious occasion for this reform was the accidental discovery, during a rebuilding of the Temple, of the Book of the Law (or Covenant). This document, found by the high priest Hilkiah, had evidently been pigeonholed and forgotten during some earlier "wicked" regime. Hilkiah's scroll is now generally supposed to have contained a basic part of the book of Deuteronomy.[12]

It was in fact at about this time that the Book of Deuteronomy seems to have taken on the form we know today. The method employed by the editor apparently was to take the older traditions, the bare bones of the Mosaic experience, the themes of national covenant and chosen people, and amplify them in terms of the prophetic tradition. The purpose was to drive home the idea that all Israel was a community bound and locked to a God who would reward those who obeyed Him and punish those who did not.

Jeremiah the prophet had supported and encouraged Josiah's reformation. But the reforms do not appear to have affected the Judean population deeply nor to have lasted long. Jeremiah found it necessary to dissociate himself from

---

[12] The problems underlying Josiah's reformation and the identification of the Book of the Covenant are very complex; see the survey article by H. H. Rowley, "The Prophet Jeremiah and the Book of Deuteronomy," in *Studies in Old Testament Prophecy* (Edinburgh, 1950), pp. 157–174.

the project and to lament its deterioration. Indeed, he went so far as to praise the piety of a small group known as the Rechabites, whose mode of living revolved about such negative principles as living in tents rather than houses and shunning the vine and its products (Jeremiah 35).

In the last years of Josiah's reign, the Assyrian empire began to crumble; by 612 the Babylonians, Medes, and Scythians had destroyed it forever and leveled its capital, the fabled Nineveh, in the dust.

This shattering event was taken by the prophet Nahum as his theme to demonstrate the retributive justice of the God of Israel. Beginning with the traditional avowal:

> The Lord is a jealous and avenging God,
>   The Lord avenges and is full of wrath;
> The Lord takes vengeance on His adversaries,
>   And He reserves wrath for His enemies. . . .

he ends his Oracle concerning Nineveh with a somber, almost elegiac, triumph:

> Your shepherds are asleep, O king of Assyria,
>   Your nobles slumber;
> Your people are scattered on the mountains,
>   And there is none to gather them.
> There is no assuaging your hurt,
>   Your wound is grievous;
> All who hear the report of you
>   Clap their hands over you.
> For upon whom has not come your evil unceasingly?

Nahum's exultation over Nineveh recalls Isaiah's epic mockery of Sennacherib almost a century before (II Kings 19:20 ff.; Isaiah 37:21 ff.).

Near Eastern Ferment and the Fall of Judah

Assyria's fall only paved the way for new and greater disasters. The Egyptians, reviving under Necho, rushed into the vacuum left by the Assyrians and made an effort to gain control of western Asia. Fearful of this threat, Josiah moved north into the valley of Jezreel to intercept the Egyptian advance. He took his stand at strategic Megiddo (about 608), but his Judean forces were overwhelmed and Josiah himself was killed (II Kings 23:29).

His son Jehoahaz II (Shallum) succeeded to the throne; but three months later Necho dragged him off in chains to the Nile and replaced him with Jehoiakim (Eliakim), another of Josiah's sons. In the meantime, however, Babylonia, the most rapidly growing power in Mesopotamia, inflicted a crushing defeat on Necho's forces at Carchemish (605) and succeeded the Assyrians as overlords of western Asia.

For a time, Jehoiakim vacillated, now looking hopefully to Babylonia, now to his Egyptian sponsors. Judah did not yet realize that Egypt would never recover from the catastrophe at Carchemish and would itself become but a dependency of other powers. Forgotten was the ancient warning: "Behold, you are putting your trust on the staff of this bruised reed, on Egypt, upon which if anyone lean, it will go into the hand and pierce it. So is Pharaoh, king of Egypt, to all who put their trust in him" (II Kings 18:21; Isaiah 36:6).

This indecision was rudely resolved when Babylonia, under the energetic leadership of the ascendant Chaldean minority headed by Nebuchadnezzar, dispatched an army that swiftly subdued all of Judah. Even then, however, Nebuchadnezzar had no sooner turned his back than Jehoiakim revolted in a desperate gamble on aid from Egypt. But even as Jeremiah had warned, this aid never came. The Chaldean conqueror replied by sending a punitive force back into Judah, and the enemy captured Jerusalem, though only after strenuous resistance.

About three months before this Babylonian expedition actually breached the city, Jehoiakim was slain, apparently the victim of a palace plot. It was his young son Jehoiachin (Jeconiah), and successor on the throne, who caught the full weight of the Babylonian vengeance. He and all the royal household, together with a portion of the upper class and a great levy of craftsmen, were marched off as captives to Babylon. As puppet ruler, the conqueror left on the throne Mattaniah, a son of Josiah, and changed his name to Zedekiah (II Kings 24:17; I Chronicles 3:15).

After some ten years of Babylonian rule, Judah revolted a second time, again refusing to heed Jeremiah's dismal warnings to rely on the Lord and not on the force of arms. This time Babylonia struck back with even greater fury, not merely to bring the rebellious province to the dust, but to dispel any dreams of like resurgence on the part of Egypt.

The Babylonians systematically took and razed all the fortified cities of Judah. Archaeological excavation has confirmed the thoroughness of this destruction. Jerusalem, the capital, held out for almost two years, but fierce hunger and the Babylonian siege engines finally broke through the defenses and forced capitulation (587–586). The conquerors leveled the Temple to the ground. "They captured the king, and brought him up to the king of Babylonia to Riblah [near Kadesh], and judgment was passed on him. They slew the sons of Zedekiah before his eyes, and put out the eyes of Zedekiah, and bound him in fetters, and took

him to Babylon" (II Kings 25:6–7). There followed renewed deportations of the people from their land. The sovereign state of Judah was no more.

Now the Babylonians reduced Judah to the status of an
outright colony, similar to that endured by Israel since the
days of the Assyrian rule. A native Judean, Gedaliah by
name, was appointed governor of the despoiled and de-
populated land and established headquarters at Mizpah.
Gedaliah's administration seems to have been mild, for many
Judeans who had fled into the hills, or into Egypt or
Transjordan, returned from their places of refuge. But a
certain Ishmael, a member of the Judean royal house, was
desirous of restoring the monarchy and, abetted by the
Ammonites, conspired to throw off Babylon's yoke. His
well-meaning but utterly irresponsible accomplices murdered Gedaliah, together with the Judeans and Babylonians
who made up his retinue, and embarked upon a reign of
terror in the land. Once again the revenge of Babylon
was swift and terrible. In 582 her troops instituted the
third and final phase of Judah's depopulation and destruction (II Kings 25; Jeremiah 41–42).

Finally peace was achieved. Judah lay quiet, all the swirl
and clash of centuries apparently come to naught. The
period of the great Babylonian Exile descended upon the
people of Judah, God's people. But the Law remained, and
all that it stood for and implied.

The Babylonian Exile
and the Restoration of Judah

THE Babylonian Exile was a supreme test of Israel's vitality. The Judeans were the only people in ancient times known to have been taken wholesale into captivity and still to have retained their religious and social identity. The Exile proved that Israel—the spiritual community—could adapt itself to, and develop under, the most adverse conditions. In fact, the very adversity seems to have bred leaders whose religious experience climaxed the prophetic tradition. Many Judeans lost faith in God. According to the Covenant He was their infallible protector; but in the contest with the Babylonian gods, He obviously had been worsted. There were others, however, who believed, also on covenantal grounds, that the Lord had visited destruction on Judah as a punishment for its wickedness; and it was this idea which was championed by the prophetic movement.

The Exile, in addition, marked the beginning of a slow transition of Judaism to a form which was destined to evolve during the period of the Second Commonwealth and set the pattern for Jewish life during the Diaspora, or great dispersion, which took place after the Romans destroyed Jerusalem in 70 A.D.

Devastation in Judah

The land of Judah, itself, lay for a time inert, physically reduced, its remnants of population bereft of direction and spirit. Recent excavations at such sites as Lachish, Bethshemesh and Tell Beit Mirsim (perhaps Kiriat-sepher) bear eloquent testimony to the devastation wreaked on the rebellious kingdom of Judah by the forces of Chaldea. In 1935 a number of *ostraca*—potsherds used as writing material— were dug up at Lachish. Most of these appear to have been military dispatches written about 588 B.C. and record a determined struggle on the part of the Judean garrisons against the more powerful Babylonian enemy. The writer of Ostracon VI expressed deep concern about rumors of defeatism among the ruling class in Jerusalem: "And behold the words of the (princes) are not good, but to weaken our hands." [1] Significantly, these relics were found buried deep in ashes.

Many towns in Judah were so thoroughly leveled by the Babylonians that they never were restored. The Temple, and the central religious organization too, was totally destroyed. The normal leaders of the community—the well-to-do, the well-educated, even the artisans—were either carried off to Babylon or fled to Transjordan and Egypt. Indeed, when Gedaliah was murdered, Jeremiah urged his fellow Judeans to remain in the land; but a group took Jeremiah forcibly with them into Egypt (Jeremiah 41–43).

As the Judean social order thus fell apart, the teachings

[1] J. Finegan, "The Lachish Letters," *Light from the Ancient Past* (Princeton, 1946), pp. 160–163, and Fig. 70.

of Moses and the sermons of the prophets were ignored and gradually forgotten. Those few remaining members of society who might have provided a nucleus of the religious and cultural stability and continuity could accomplish almost nothing in the chaotic conditions which prevailed. Edomites, Ammonites, Moabites, and others from the neighboring regions—some of whom had previously been settled by Assyria in the territory of the northern kingdom —encroached more and more on the territory of Judah. Inevitably this infiltration led to intermarriage with these alien peoples and then indirectly their gradually increasing influence upon the religious practices and daily life of the Israelites. Thus with the general tendency toward social and intellectual deterioration, assimilation and syncretism went on apace. Finally Judah, much reduced in territory, came under the control of a governor who resided in Samaria.

The Babylonian Captivity

In Babylonia, the exiled Jews found themselves in the midst of a flourishing and impressive civilization. The Chaldean regime of Nebuchadnezzar (605–562)—currently the greatest power in western Asia—had embarked on a tremendous building campaign for the glorification of the king, his capital, and his empire. Among the new structures were the terraces of Babylon, the so-called Hanging Gardens which the Greeks made famous as one of the seven wonders of the world. In actual fact, these masonry terraces were eclipsed by the Ishtar Gate and by the temple of Marduk built in stepped tiers like the towers of a modern skyscraper. To carry out these projects, artisans of all kinds were imported, both as captives and as highly paid skilled

workers, as recorded in the Biblical statement: "And Nebuchadnezzar carried away . . . all the craftsmen and smiths"
(II Kings 24:14).

The Judean exiles were treated no differently from the
other captive peoples. The common folk were generally
enslaved outright, and those of higher status were given
limited freedom to earn a living and choose their abode.
A number of the exiled Judeans even managed to live in their
own homes in a special quarter of the city of Babylon.

Especially interesting is the manner in which the Biblical
and the Babylonian texts confirm and clarify one another in
their statements about the Babylonian treatment of King
Jehoiachin and his household. The Biblical historian tells
us:

And in the thirty-seventh year of the exile of Jehoiachin king
of Judah . . . Evil-merodach king of Babylon, in the year that
he began to reign, lifted up the head of Jehoiachin king of Judah
from prison. And he spoke kindly to him, and gave him a seat
above the seats of the kings who were with him in Babylon.
And Jehoiachin put off his prison garments, and he ate regularly
in the king's presence all the days of his life. And for his allowance, a regular allowance was given him by the king, every day
a portion, all the days of his life [II Kings 25:27–30].

Shortly after the beginning of the twentieth century, the
Kaiser's Museum in Berlin received some three hundred
cuneiform tablets which had been excavated by a German
expedition near the Ishtar Gate in Babylon. These tablets
lay for over three decades in the basement of the museum,
uncleaned and undeciphered. Under the very thorough
Nazi regime, the curator of the museum came upon the
boxes of tablets and began to study them. He was astounded
to discover that several of the tablets dealt precisely with

this same King Jehoiachin of Judah and his family in exile in Babylon, and that these texts not only substantiated but even filled in gaps in the Biblical account. It is unusual for archaeological discoveries to confirm a Biblical account so specifically.[2]

Practically all the Judean exiles, except those who had been enslaved and brutalized by exhausting manual labor, longed for home. As time passed, however, and no immediate prospect of release developed, many were caught up in the colorful life of the Babylonian metropolis. These practical folk, recognizing that life went on in any case, made up their minds to "sing low in a bad tune," and to learn to adjust to Babylonian ways and customs according to the advice of Jeremiah:

Thus says the Lord of Hosts, the God of Israel, to all the exiles whom I have exiled from Jerusalem to Babylon: Build yourselves houses, and dwell in them, and plant gardens, and eat their fruit. Take yourselves wives and have sons and daughters; and take wives for your sons, and give your daughters to husbands, that they may bear sons and daughters; and multiply there and be not diminished. And seek the welfare of the city to which I have exiled you, and pray to the Lord for it; for in its welfare shall you have welfare [29:4 ff.].

It should be noted in passing that Jeremiah did not give the Babylonians any credit for having overpowered Judah. The Lord, having condemned Judah, delivered her people to Babylon to serve out their sentence of exile. Thus, according to Jeremiah, the only thing to do was to endure the captivity and build up a record for good behavior.

By about the middle of the sixth century, after some three

[2] See W. F. Albright, "King Joiachin in Exile," *Biblical Archaeologist*, V (Dec., 1942), 49–55.

or four decades, two generations of Judeans had grown up in exile. Those born to families that had sought assimilation had quite lost touch with Judah. For them the memory of Temple and Covenant had faded, and Jerusalem seemed remote and unimportant compared with mighty and cosmopolitan Babylon. Content to earn a living in peace, these people had no desire to return to the land of their fathers and grandfathers.

A minority of the exiles, however, did remain faithful. Consisting largely of priests, Levites, men of learning, landowners, functionaries of the royal administration, and the like, this group maintained the will to resist assimilation. They struggled to keep track of political developments in the world about them and to keep alive the dream of restoring the Temple and the nation of Judah. For them captivity was bitter frustration, and deliverance and return held the one great promise of life, a hope which they implanted and nursed in their children with religious fervor.

The voices of the prophets ceaselessly and tirelessly admonished the expatriates always to remember their origin, their faith, and their mission. These faithful few did not intermarry, or at least not in sufficient numbers to dilute their consciousness of kind. They studied the teachings of Moses and the prophets, and found in them not only the explanation of Judah's defeat and exile, but also a program for salvation and redemption.

The Prophet Ezekiel

Among the Biblical writings which gave expression to this belief, the foremost were the books of Ezekiel and the so-called Second Isaiah. Ezekiel, the first prophet to receive the divine call outside the Holy Land, was visited by God

Himself in a vision in Babylonia, and commanded to preach that Judah and the Temple had been overcome not by the might of Babylon, but by the wickedness of Judah which had provoked God's wrath.

Carrying on the great tradition of Jeremiah, Ezekiel contended that the God of Israel was still omnipotent and that Babylon was His mere instrument. Her pomp and might, her lion-guarded ways, her many gods who were "no-gods," all these trappings and appurtenances of power would vanish like mist, once God's anger had run its course. Ezekiel would tolerate no momentary doubt of the inflexible justice of his God, nor would he accept the possibility that God would allow the innocent among the exiled to languish forever and without hope in the same durance with the wicked. With the same fiery faith Ezekiel preached that this punishment that made the bad good, made the good better, and assured, at least ultimately, deliverance for all who obeyed the Lord, observed His Sabbath, and kept themselves from heathen idols and heathen ways.

Ezekiel propounded his basic convictions in the vision of the Valley of Dry Bones (Ezekiel 37), one of the most electrifying passages of the entire Bible. Israel—in this vision —had ceased to be a living nation. Her people had lost faith in God and in themselves. To dramatize their plight, Ezekiel likened them to scattered heaps of bleached bone, lying in a valley. But the Lord, who had brought this terrible curse on His people, promised to bring the dead bones to life, and to restore a unified Israel to its own land under a descendant of King David, saying: "And I will make a covenant of peace with them, and it shall be an everlasting covenant with them; and I will establish them and multiply them, and will set My sanctuary in their midst for ever.

. . . And the nations shall know that I the Lord sanctify Israel, when My sanctuary is in their midst for ever" (verses 26–28).

Ezekiel, the first to prophesy after the destruction of Jerusalem, was obsessed by the need to rebuild the Temple. As the abode of the Divine Presence, it was the center of Israelite religious life, the true setting for sacrifice and prayer, for in antiquity no less than nowadays, organized religion required a special place for the worship of the Deity.[3] It was natural, therefore, that Ezekiel should also stress the preservation of a strict observance of the Temple ritual. In absolute accord with such exilic and postexilic prophets as the Second Isaiah, Haggai, Zechariah, and Malachi, not to mention his pre-exilic predecessors, Ezekiel warned that ritual laxity led to moral laxity. He and the other prophets of this later era were by no means men of coarser fiber; on the contrary, all of them believed—as firmly as their predecessors—that the efficacy of prayer and sacrifice depended on the worshipper's religious integrity. Their insistence on sacred forms and symbols stemmed not from a willingness to substitute such external tokens for the deeper religious truths but—on the contrary —from their experience that it is infinitely difficult for ordinary men to maintain active religious belief by faith alone.

The Second Isaiah: Babylonian Decline

Ezekiel had never faltered in his convictions of deliverance even during the worst hours of the Exile, but he did

---

[3] Cf. the famous prayer of dedication of Solomon's Temple (I Kings 8:22–53; II Chronicles 6:12–40), and the symposium on "The Significance of the Temple in the Ancient Near East" cited above in chapter iii, n. 3.

not live to see his faith vindicated. Only a few decades after Ezekiel's career came to a close, however, the Babylonian empire began to show great cracks and fissures, and in shorter time than anyone would have believed possible, was on the brink of dissolution. The Persians and Medes had begun to take their place as major powers in the Mesopotamian region late in the seventh century. First the Medes helped the Babylonians crush Assyria and shared in the spoils. Then, about 545, Persia under Cyrus II (the Great) of the Achemenid dynasty absorbed Media, Lydia, and Ionian Greece in Asia Minor. Eventually the new power was to include territories extending all the way from the Indus to the Mediterranean, and from the Caucasus to the Indian Ocean, a dominion beside which the conquests of earlier Near Eastern empires pale into insignificance.

During this turbulent period, a great prophet arose to proclaim to his fellow Jews in Babylon that they were entering a new epoch. He is called nowadays the "Second" Isaiah, to distinguish him from the namesake who prophesied in Jerusalem some two hundred years earlier; the writings of this exilic prophet are found in Chapters 40–66 of the Book of Isaiah. They are easily differentiated from those of the First Isaiah by virtue of literary style, historical perspective, and theological emphasis.

Having followed political developments closely, the Second Isaiah realized that even greater events were in the making, and in the swift rise of Persia he sensed the promise of imminent deliverance for Israel. In poetic sermons rarely equaled for pathos and lyricism, he compared the Babylonian Exile with Israel's bondage in Egypt, and urged his conviction that even the Exodus would be surpassed by the new liberation and return, a triumph that would be consecrated in a new covenant between God and His people Israel. The one necessary condition, the unknown prophet of the Exile warned, was that the Judean exiles have complete faith in the ability and desire of the Lord to accomplish the restoration.

More than any other prophet since the days of Elijah, the Second Isaiah emphasized and reiterated the uniqueness and omnipotence of the God of Israel. He set himself the task of convincing his fellow Jews that the Babylonians and their gods were not victors over the Judeans and the Lord their God, but that, on the contrary, the heathen were no more than the rod of His anger and chastisement. God was the one ruler in the entire universe, and there was no one else beside Him:

> I am the Lord, that is My name,
> And My glory I will not give to another
> Nor My praise to graven images [42:8].

This concept of a universal and omnipotent God was new, of course, only in emphasis. It stemmed in direct line from the teachings of Elijah and Amos, and had been eloquently expressed by the otherwise unknown "man of God" who said to King Ahab of Israel (ninth century), "Thus says the Lord: Because the Arameans have said, 'The Lord is a God of the mountains, but He is not a God of the valleys,' therefore I will deliver all this great multitude into your hand, and you shall know that I am the Lord" (I Kings 20:28). But as Ezekiel stressed the role of the lost Temple in the worship of the Lord and made its rebuilding a central object of faith, so the Second Isaiah emphasized the universal aspect of God, in his efforts to explain to his fellow Judeans their exile in the foreign land of a great empire which had destroyed the Temple of their God and carried them captive from His land.

The Second Isaiah, realizing that Babylonia was a mere shell of its former greatness, and that Persia was now the dominant power in the Near East, warned his listeners that they had little time to prepare themselves for the destruction of Babylon by God's "shepherd" and "anointed," Cyrus of Persia (Isaiah 44:28; 45:1), and for their liberation and return to Judah.

Cyrus of Persia and the Edict of Liberation

About 540 B.C. Babylonia fell like a ripe fruit into the hands of Persia's king. In his first regnal year (about 538) Cyrus issued the famous Edict of Liberation: "Thus says Cyrus king of Persia: All the kingdoms of the earth has the Lord, the God of heaven, given me; and He has charged me to build Him a house in Jerusalem, which is in Judah. Whosoever there is among you of all His people—his God be with him—let him go up to Jerusalem" (Ezra 1:2-3; II Chronicles 36:22-23). And he added:

Concerning the house of God at Jerusalem, let the house be built, the place where they offer sacrifices, and let its foundation be strongly laid. Its height shall be sixty cubits, and its width sixty cubits, with three rows of great stones and a row of new timber; and let the expenses be paid out of the king's house. And also let the gold and silver vessels of the house of God, which Nebuchadnezzar took out of the Temple which is in Jerusalem and brought to Babylon, be restored and brought back to the Temple which is in Jerusalem, every one to its place. And you shall put them in the house of God [Ezra 6:3-5].

Sheshbazzar, apparently of the family of King Jehoiachin of Judah, was appointed governor of Judah. Taking with him the sacred vessels of the Temple, Sheshbazzar went to Jerusalem to take up his post, and prepared to lay the foundations for the new Temple.

Developments in Judah

But the Judean homeland, devastated and impoverished by Babylonia, was in no condition to support a significant restoration. Many Judeans in Babylonia failed to take advantage of the new liberty to return to Judah. The majority, having adapted themselves well enough to their new home, lacked the necessary incentive to start all over again in a much poorer land. As for the many who had never been forced into exile, few evinced any enthusiasm for rebuilding the Temple and for recapturing a way of life long since abandoned. Nearly twenty years after Cyrus' edict, the prophet Haggai condemned the Judeans for their inertia, saying bitterly, "Is it a time for you yourselves to dwell in your paneled houses, while this house lies in ruins?" (1:4). When drought and famine came upon the land, Haggai insisted that the hardships were a manifestation of God's displeasure at the people's failure to rebuild His Temple. The prophet Zechariah, too, castigated the people for their apathy.

The foreigners who had poured into Judah during the Exile saw the restoration of the Temple as a threat to their position and prosperity, and, accordingly, opposed it. Among those of mixed marriages, the attitudes ranged from complete indifference to a willingness to back the projects; but when some of this mixed population, chiefly the Samaritans, volunteered their assistance, their offer was rejected and they were denounced as idolaters (Ezra 4:1-4, 24; 5-6).

During this period, Zerubbabel, of the family of King

Jehoiachin and the House of David, was the civil head of
the community, and Joshua the high priest was recognized
leader of the priestly group. Haggai and Zechariah had
envisaged a restoration of Judah under a scion of the House
of David, with a free priesthood in full charge of the Temple and religious matters.

It was, however, the representatives of the religious rather
than the civil authority who finally came to power. Cam-
byses II, son and successor of Cyrus, committed suicide in
522 B.C., and for a brief interval the Persian empire faltered.
During the confusion, several of the subject provinces revolted, creating the impression among some of the Judeans
still at home—Haggai and Zechariah among them—that the
end of the empire was at hand. Jumping at what they took
to be a chance to restore Judah's independence at one blow,
they named Zerubbabel God's chosen one, thus declaring
independence of Persia (Haggai 2:20-23). The priestly
group seems to have been more cautious. And their cau-
tion was rewarded when Darius I (522-486 B.C.), crushed
the widespread rebellion, and re-established the imperial
rule.

Just how Zerubbabel and his backers fared during this
troubled interlude is not known, but the movement is never
heard of again. Led by Haggai and Joshua, however, the
Judeans persevered in their efforts to rebuild the Temple.
The Persian government, in accordance with its general
policy of supporting local priesthoods, ignored the objec-
tions of its own governor, Tattenai, and of the anti-Jewish
section of the population, and granted the Jews permission
to continue with the work. About 516 B.C. the second Temple was dedicated, just seventy years after the first had been

destroyed. Judah now became a theocracy, under Persian rule, with Joshua the high priest at its head.

Little is known about the happenings in Judea during the earlier part of the fifth century. The Persian government continued its policy of granting its colonies, Judea included, a considerable degree of religious and cultural autonomy, keeping at the same time a firm hold on military, economic, and political affairs. The Jewish community in Judea grew in numbers and in prosperity only gradually, and while it seems to have taken good care of the Temple, it permitted the walls of Jerusalem, destroyed by Nebuchadnezzar's army, to remain in ruins. At the same time, intermarriage between the Judeans and the gentiles continued, and their assimilation progressed.

The Jewries of Egypt and Persia

Elsewhere in the Persian empire Jews were involved in two revealing incidents. It will be remembered that when Nebuchadnezzar's forces were overrunning Judah, and again when the Judeans revolted—to their sorrow—against Gedaliah, some of the populace sought asylum in Egypt. About sixty years later (c. 525 B.C.) the Persians incorporated Egypt in their empire, whereupon some of the expatriate Jews there volunteered for military service with the conqueror, and were assigned to garrison duty.

The sudden reappearance of Jews in Egyptian history is recorded by the Elephantine Papyri, ancient documents of a Jewish military colony at the city of Elephantine, just below the first cataract of the Nile. Written in Aramaic —the "language of diplomacy and trade throughout Western Asia in the Persian period, and which was gradually replacing Hebrew as the everyday tongue of the Jewish people not only abroad, but also at home in Palestine" [4]— the Elephantine Papyri constitute a prime source for the reconstruction of Egyptian and Jewish history and throw important side lights on the colonial history of Persia as well. They indicate, for example, that the imperial rule of the Persian government was generally liberal, at least in comparison with the naked despotism of her predecessors, Egypt, Babylon, and Assyria.

The Jewish colony was allowed its own temple where sacrifices were regularly offered up to God and around which the colony's activities revolved. The business contracts and other documents among the Papyri indicate that the Jews bought and sold land and houses, married and divorced, and, in general, lived a normal life. There is evidence that some Jews intermarried with the Egyptians and became more or less assimilated in the religious and social life of the country. The community as a whole, however, appears to have retained a distinct character. For one thing, it was organized along military lines, with Persians and Babylonians normally in command of the larger units. Then too, the Jews, unlike the native Egyptians, employed Aramaic as their official language. Finally the Jewish colonists, genuinely appreciative of the Persian colonial policy and their privileged position in the imperial organization, were the most loyal subjects that Persia had.

On several occasions the Egyptians revolted against their Persian conquerors. In one of these uprisings, during the

[4] Finegan, *op. cit.*, p. 201. And see now the article by E. G. Kraeling on the recently identified Elephantine Papyri in the Brooklyn Museum, shedding "New Light on the Elephantine Colony," *Biblical Archaeologist*, XV (Sept., 1952), 50–67; also his edition of *The Brooklyn Museum Aramaic Papyri* (New Haven, 1953).

reign of Darius II (about 410), a mob incited by the local priests and merchants attacked and looted the Jewish temple in the first anti-Jewish pogrom on record. The motivation behind this directed outburst of violence—which the Persian authorities quickly suppressed and punished—appears to have been a combination of two related factors. First, the Egyptian upper classes sought to divert the social discontent among the general population against an alien religious group which could also be identified with Persian imperialism. Second, the Egyptian priests and merchants hoped to exploit the general social discontent to weaken and, if possible, to destroy their economic rivals in the Jewish community.

The Book of Esther describes a similar incident, this time at Susa, at the eastern end of the Persian empire. A certain Haman, the highest official in the regime of King Ahasuerus —perhaps one of the Xerxes kings—persuaded his master to hand over to him for destruction and spoil the Jews of Susa and of the empire. Haman pointed out that the Jews were unassimilable, and that "their laws are diverse from those of every people" (Esther 3:8). Indeed, Haman argued, it was "not to the king's profit to tolerate them," and for the privilege of stripping them—which would be a public service—he offered to pay ten thousand talents of silver. In spite of the extraordinary offer Haman was thwarted by Ahasuerus' favorite, the Jewess Esther (Hadassah). Under the guidance of her wise cousin, Mordecai, she caused Haman to be hanged from his own gallows and his henchmen killed. But the Jews, in their turn, "did not stretch forth their hand to the spoil" of the Persians (3:11, 13; 9:15–16).

The Book of Esther, as so many critics have pointed out,

is much too pat and wishfully contrived to be accepted as simple historical fact. Yet the account, however much idealized, follows closely, in essence, the objective chronicle of the Elephantine Papyri, and may therefore safely be considered as a reflection of fact. It seems more than likely that under the Achemenid regime expatriate Jews achieved positions of wealth and influence, not only in Egypt but throughout the Persian empire, and that this personal prosperity produced the usual inimical repercussions engendered by minority success—which would account for the story of Esther, or pogrom narrowly averted.

Among the Jews, the triumph of Esther came to be observed in the joyous feast of Purim, which recalls "the days wherein the Jews had rest from their enemies, and the month was turned for them from sorrow to gladness, and from mourning to a good day; that they should make them days of feasting and gladness, and of sending choice portions one to another, and gifts to the poor" (9:22). After the destruction of Judah and the Temple, and the subsequent exile, it was natural for a people to celebrate joyfully such a narrow and triumphant escape from great disaster.

Ezra and Nehemiah

To return to Judah—or Judea, to keep its new status clear—the decisive turn toward national as well as religious revival came about in the time of Ezra the Scribe and Nehemiah. Just when Ezra lived is unknown—even whether he preceded, was contemporary with, or followed Nehemiah. But their combined influence on the history of Judea during the latter half of the fifth and the first decades of the fourth centuries is made abundantly clear in the Biblical text.

V. The restoration under Ezra and Nehemiah (fifth and fourth centuries B.C.).

An important person in the Jewish community of Babylon and highly regarded by the Persian government, Ezra, "the priest and scribe of the Law of the God of heaven," was authorized by King Artaxerxes to proceed to Jerusalem, and there, with the assistance of the king's officials, to reorganize the entire Jewish community in accordance with the Law of Moses (Ezra 7:12–26).

Ezra brought back with him to Judea the various compilations which recorded the early traditions of the patriarchal and Mosaic period, substantially the Five Books of Moses as preserved today. Chapter 8 of Nehemiah describes the dramatic scene in Jerusalem when the entire adult Jewish population gathered to hear Ezra read and explain to them the text of the Torah, the Law of Moses. Rabbi Jose of Palestine (second century A.D.) justly expressed the importance of Ezra, even in comparison with Moses, in the establishment of the Torah as the basis of Judaism, when he said, "Ezra was worthy of having the Law given through him to Israel, had not Moses preceded him." [5]

One of the important consequences of the official adoption of the Torah, in addition to the renewed observance of such holy days as the feasts of Tabernacles (Succoth) and Passover, was the decision of Ezra to order every Jew to divorce his gentile wife. This was a far-reaching decision, and not an easy one to carry out. Opposition to this move came from every walk of Jewish life, and it found expression in the Book of Ruth. The author of this beautiful little novel expressed the opinion that no gentile who

[5] Babylonian Talmud, Tractate Sanhedrin, folio 21b bottom. It is the opinion of some scholars that Ezra is the author of the Book of Chronicles; this is problematical.

became a sincere convert to Judaism, such as Ruth the Moabitess, should be cast out or denied.

This attitude would not ordinarily have been rejected; but in this period intermarriage had become so extensive, and the consequences so detrimental to the Jews as God's people, that Ezra and his followers could no longer accept the results in silence. It should be noted, in this connection, too, that the author of Ruth did not favor Judean missionary activity among the gentiles. Biblical Israel was not evangelical, and genuine voluntary conversion to Judaism was at most condoned.

While maintaining the policy of continued loyalty to Persia, Ezra led a social and religious revival in Judea. At about this time some Jews began to rebuild the walls of Jerusalem. This prompted the governor of Samaria, under whose administration Judea lay, to notify King Artaxerxes that the Jews were planning to revolt. The king at once ordered the work stopped. Nehemiah, a loyal cup-bearer in the royal court and an ardent Zionist, hearing of the order, pleaded to be allowed to supervise the work himself, vowing that he would proceed in such a way that the imperial interest would not be jeopardized. "If it please the king," he begged, "and if your servant has found favor in your sight, send me to Judah, to the city of my fathers' sepulchres, that I may build it" (Nehemiah 2:5).

Artaxerxes was persuaded, and Nehemiah went to Judea taking with him full credentials and authority. As would be expected, Nehemiah's extraordinary powers aroused bitter opposition in Judea. Sanballat, governor of Samaria and Nehemiah's superior, and Tobiah, governor of Ammon, accused Nehemiah of plotting a revolt against the king.

Geshem the Arab, perhaps the governor of Dedan in Arabia, "whom it grieved greatly that someone had come to seek the welfare of the children of Israel" (2:10), also took umbrage. Geshem became embroiled in the Judean situation because of his fear of a commercial revival to the north, which would have put him back in the same disadvantageous position that Arabia's Queen of Sheba had occupied in relation to Israel's King Solomon.

Nehemiah, however, was not deterred, nor did the Persian central government withdraw its support. The walls of Jerusalem, the Bible tells us, were restored in fifty-two days of heroic effort, as Nehemiah had boasted would happen in his prophetic defiance: "The God of heaven will succeed for us; and we His servants, we will arise and we will build. And you will have no portion or right or memorial in Jerusalem" (2:20). The builders "did the work with one hand and held a weapon in the other," we are told in a passage (Nehemiah 4:11ff.; 4:17 ff. in the English versions) that recalls the rebuilding of modern Israel.

As had so often happened before in Judea, improving fortune brought a corresponding increase of social inequity. Once again the upper-class Judeans enriched themselves at the expense of the poor. The moneylenders tightened their fists, the common folk began to lose their land and property, serfdom reappeared. "We are forcing our sons and daughters to become slaves," the people complained to Nehemiah: "Some of our daughters have been enslaved, and we cannot help it, for other men possess our fields and our vineyards" (5:1 ff.).[6]

---

[6] See in general, I. Mendelsohn, *Slavery in the Ancient Near East* (New York, 1949), ch. i, §7 "Insolvency," pp. 23 ff.; ch. ii, §9 "Manumission," pp. 74 ff.

The heavy tribute paid to Persia by Judea further aggravated the situation because the well-to-do industriously foisted onto the common people as large a share as possible of this collective obligation. To correct the serious dislocation, Nehemiah attempted to force the rich to take an oath guaranteeing the return of mortgaged properties and goods held under pledge to their owners. This act of social justice, which may possibly have been a political move to win mass support for the theocratic party, provoked the Persian overseers to recall Nehemiah to Shushan, where he cooled his heels for some twelve years.

During his absence, religious conditions in Jerusalem deteriorated. Tobiah the Ammonite had set up living quarters in the court of the Temple. Many of the levitical and priestly workers had left the Temple because they were not being supported by its revenues. The Sabbath was being violated, by Jews as well as by local Tyrian merchants. Intermarriage between Jews and the gentile populations of Ashdod, Ammon, and Moab again increased, and the children were being raised in ignorance of their Jewish faith and of the Hebrew language.

When the zealot, Nehemiah, finally returned to Jerusalem, he wasted no time in throwing out Tobiah. He appointed honest treasurers, and restored the Temple staff to full complement. Breakers of the Sabbath laws were arrested and punished. And those who dared flout the ban on intermarriage were fined, cursed, and made to take an oath that never would they permit their issue to marry a gentile. Nehemiah ended his remarkable memoirs with the plea, "Remember me, O my God, for good."

The Jewish Theocratic State

The historical legacy of Ezra and Nehemiah was the theocratic state of Judea. In graphic form, it may be described as follows:

The Persian Royal Administration   The Law of Moses

High Priest of Judah

Administrative   Judges   Temple
Bureaucracy   Administration

The urban and rural population, especially the peasantry, who supported the entire structure and accepted the Mosaic Law and priestly control, in the belief that their well-being was thus assured.

The Jewish theocratic state was strong enough to withstand the various forces of opposition, both domestic and international, which beset her. Thus Sanballat of Samaria built a temple on Mount Gerizim for his son-in-law, Manasseh, grandson of Eliashib the high priest of Jerusalem. This Samaritan shrine and its adherents became in time a festering sore to the Jews of Judea.

The administrative and religious bureaucracies fought constantly for power. On one occasion (about 400), Bagoas, the governor of Judea, threatened to dismiss Jonathan, the high priest, in favor of the latter's brother, Joshua. Jonathan murdered Joshua in the Temple, and Bagoas used this as a pretext to interfere with the Temple services and the priestly prerogatives.

A pattern of Judaism was being woven in Judea while the Persian empire at large was beginning to show signs of disintegration. The history of the Jewish people, shaped largely by the priests during the rest of the Persian period, was soon to enter a new stage, in the Hellenistic period, when the theocratic state was replaced by a commonwealth, and when the Torah constitution was reinterpreted by the liberal Pharisees in accordance with the new conditions. The Judaism which the Pharisees developed maintained a profound influence on all phases of Jewish life during the more than two thousand years which followed and is a potent factor in Judaism and in Israel today.

The Hebraic Spirit: The Prophetic Movement and Social Justice

THE prophetic movement forms the climax of Biblical history. Not only was nothing comparable produced by any of the other Near Eastern civilizations of antiquity, but not even the heirs of the Hebraic tradition itself again equaled the power and eloquence of this great moral outburst. Moreover, its influence has followed the spread of, and dominated the development of, the three great world religions, Judaism, Christianity, and Islam, to such extent that for twenty centuries, over nearly half the land surface of the globe, the consciences of civilized men have spoken with the accents of the prophets. The atheistic socialists of the nineteenth century, who scorned all revealed religion, acknowledged the prophets as the first social reformers and the source of their own new doctrine.[1] Even rationalist and skeptical scholars of the period, who rejected nearly every part of the Bible as unhistorical, recognized the greatness

[1] See, e.g., "Palestine," ch. i. of M. Beer, *Social Struggles in Antiquity* (Boston, no date); H. W. Laidler, *A History of Socialist Thought* (New York, 1933). It is erroneous, however, to list the prophets among the utopians, as Laidler, among others, has done.

of the prophets, the validity of their teaching, and the power of their eloquence.[2]

The Rise of the Prophetic Movement

The Hebrew word for "prophet" is *nabi*, but its original meaning is not known. It would seem that *nabi* in the Bible meant approximately "spokesman," as when the Lord told Moses, "Aaron your brother shall be your spokesman" (Exodus 7:1; and compare the parallel statement in 4:16). That is how the Jews themselves translated *nabi* in the oldest Greek translation of the Pentateuch, the Septuagint, about 200 B.C.; and the Greek word which was there employed, *prophētēs*, "declarer" or "interpreter," is the source of the English word "prophet." Indeed, it appears that the word "prophet" in English, at least until the time of Queen Elizabeth, meant simply "forthteller," or "preacher"; the meaning "foretelling," "predicting," is a later development.[3] The prophet spoke for God, and interpreted His word and will to his fellow Israelites.

The prophetic movement in Israel developed in two distinct stages. In the earlier phase, the Biblical prophets were essentially no different from the diviners common to the ancient Near East in general. In fact, the Bible itself states explicitly, in an editorial gloss at I Samuel 9:9, "Previously in Israel, when a person went to inquire of God, thus he said, 'Come, let us go to the seer'; for he who is now called a prophet was previously called a seer." Samuel the prophet

---

[2] See the useful summary, "The Nature of Old Testament Prophecy in the Light of Recent Study," ch. iii of H. H. Rowley, *The Servant of the Lord and Other Essays on the Old Testament* (London, 1952).

[3] According to T. J. Meek, *Hebrew Origins*, rev. ed. (New York, 1950), p. 151.

was called a "seer" and "a man of God." And in II Samuel
24:11 we read that "the word of the Lord came to the
prophet Gad, David's visionary [or, seer]."

Soothsayers, seers, miracle workers—that is, people who
divined by magic formula, who gave out oracular utter-
ances, who professed expertness in transmitting the supernatural—were a definite social group in the ancient
civilizations of the Near East. Ecstasy, frenzy, the examination of the liver and entrails of animals, the flight of birds,
the interpretation of dreams, astrology, the casting of lots,
divination by water—all these were the property and trade-
mark of the priestly and related guilds from the Euphrates
to the Nile. For the seers of antiquity were organized in
guilds, which had set rules governing masters and apprentices, as surely as if they were stonemasons. These craftsmen in the supernatural worked both in groups and as
individuals.

Cuneiform texts recently discovered at Mari, dating from
the eighteenth century B.C., illustrate this earlier stage in
Biblical prophecy. They describe how a deputation of
priests advises the king to pay more attention to the gods
that they represent, and to the sanctuary that they make
it their business to tend.[4] Another text, this one from Egypt
and dating back to about 1100 B.C., illustrates how holy
men resorted to states of frenzy in order to "divine." This
text tells us that when the king of Byblos "was sacrificing
to his gods, the god seized one of his great boys and made

---

[4] Cf., e.g., M. Noth, in *Bulletin of the John Rylands Library*,
XXXII (March, 1950), 194–206; A. Lods, in *Studies in Old Testament Prophecy*, ed. H. H. Rowley (Edinburgh, 1950), pp. 103–
110; W. von Soden, in *Die Welt des Orients* (1950), pp. 397–403.
These articles have erred in connecting the Mari texts with the
later, uniquely Israelite phase of prophecy.

him frenzied. And he said to him, 'Bring up the god! Bring
up the messenger who is carrying him! It is Amon who has
sent him; he it is who made him come!' " [5]

Divine seizures and frenzies are reported of Biblical
prophecy in its formative stage, often in a context which
suggests the existence of recognized soothsayer or seer
groups specializing in the invocation of hysterical trances.
For example, shortly after Saul was anointed king by Samuel, he ran into a "band of prophets coming down from the
shrine, led by harp, tambourine, flute, and lyre . . . and
the spirit of God rushed upon him, and he prophesied among
them" (I Samuel 10:5–12). In fact, it seems probable that
the early prophets were all to some degree professional
soothsayers. Several, Nathan, Gad, and Iddo, for example,
were attached to the royal court, just as the priests, the
tax-collectors, the commander-in-chief of the army, and
other royal functionaries. Others, like Samuel of Ramah and
Ahijah of Shiloh, were attached to sanctuaries outside of
Jerusalem; and in this early stage, they frequently worked
in groups. Samuel himself was head of such a "band of
prophets" as Saul had met (19:20). When Jezebel murdered "the prophets of the Lord," one of her officials,
Obadiah, saved the lives of one hundred of them (I Kings
18:4). In the days of Elijah and Elisha there is frequent
mention of groups of prophets of the Lord, among them
the groups located at Jericho and Bethel.[6] On another occasion four hundred "prophets of the Lord" were summoned
by Jehoshaphat of Judah and the king of Israel to interpret

[5] J. A. Wilson, in *Ancient Near Eastern Texts*, ed. J. B. Pritchard
(Princeton, 1950), p. 26. Wilson notes, "The determinative [sign]
of the word for (prophetically) possessed [or frenzied] shows a
human figure in violent motion or epileptic convulsion."

[6] Cf., e.g., I Kings 20:35 ff.; 22:6, 10; II Kings 2:3, 5; 4:1; 6:1.

God's will in regard to an attack on Ramoth-gilead (I Kings 22:6). This incident recalls the 450 prophets of Baal and the 400 prophets of Asherah who contested with Elijah's God on Mount Carmel (I Kings 18).

Among the earlier prophets, it was also characteristic to transmit the art from generation to generation. Elijah trained Elisha and invested him as his successor (II Kings 2, a dramatic chapter), and before them, Jehu the prophet was the father of Hanani the seer (I Kings 16:1,7; II Chronicles 16:7–10). Likewise, nearly all performed miracles, as Moses did before Pharaoh to convince him that the God of the Hebrews was supreme. Samuel was a seer; and the prophets Elijah and Elisha freely worked miracles of various kinds.

From Miracle to Rhapsody

In the eighth century, however, divination and miracle working were virtually eliminated from the prophetic tradition in Israel. Seers such as Samuel and miracle workers like Elijah and Elisha ceased to be the norm. The ecstatic element continued, but the prophets began to utilize and perfect another medium by which to convince their fellow Israelites of the truth of their teachings. To achieve this effect they began to rely more and more on the eloquence and logic of their literary compositions.

The development from the miracle-working to the rhapsodic stage of prophecy was not peaceful and evolutionary. The literary prophets were opposed to the prophetic guilds, to the practice of prophecy as a craft, and to the idea that any person could be taught by the masters how to "prophesy."

There is no evidence that any of the later literary prophets functioned in groups or that they were heads or members of guilds or that they produced disciples. They were not representatives of any court or sanctuary, nor did they practice prophecy as a regular occupation or a way to earn a living. Instead, they felt themselves inspired directly by God, and only when God and the occasion demanded, as Amos insisted (in the eighth century): "For the Lord God does nothing without revealing His counsel to His servants the prophets. . . . The Lord God has spoken, who can help but prophesy!" (3:7–8). Thus when the chief priest at Bethel contemptuously dismissed Amos and told him to go back to his native Judah to make a living there from his craft, Amos was stung to protest, "I am not a [professional] prophet nor a member of a prophetic guild [literally, the son of a prophet]; but I am a herdsman, and a dresser of sycamore trees" (7:12 ff.). In time, the literary prophets came to scorn the priests—who had become little more than functionaries of the royal court—and the various groups of prophets—whom they called "false prophets"—and they saw only themselves as the true spokesmen of God.

It should not be overlooked that several of the earlier prophets had produced important literary compositions. Thus we are told in I Chronicles 29:29: "The acts of King David, first and last, are written in the account of Samuel the seer, and the account of Nathan the prophet, and the account of Gad the visionary." Similar accounts of Solomon's reign were written by the prophets Nathan and Ahijah, of Jeroboam's reign by Iddo the seer, and of Jehoshaphat's reign by Jehu the seer (II Chronicles 9:29; 20:34).

Nevertheless, the later prophets fully merit the characterization of "literary" or "rhapsodic," to distinguish them from their predecessors.[7] This title, however, must not be allowed to obscure the far more important fact that this elevation of style reflects a sublimated moral and religious experience, free from the least trace of magic. It is this sublimated character which most fundamentally distinguishes the "literary" prophets from their precursors. Amos, Isaiah, Jeremiah, and the others, unlike Ahijah, Elijah, or Jehu, had a broad understanding of the historical situation in which they lived, and their formulations were strikingly eloquent. In the great poetic sermons of the literary prophets, the differences of degree unmistakably merge into a significant difference of kind.

All the later prophets—Amos, Hosea, Joel, Isaiah, Zechariah, the Second Isaiah, and so on—transmitted God's word directly to the people. Such "men of God," who were also "men of the hour," are unknown anywhere in the ancient world except in Israel. They were independent personalities, quite unconnected with any vested religious interest, archaic or otherwise. Formal religionists came seeking them, never the reverse.

The Prophetic Concept of Social Justice: The Covenant and the Law

The prophets, the earlier as well as the later, took their stand on two fundamental ideas: first, that there was a covenant between God and His people Israel, and second, that this covenant bound the Israelites to a completely ethical relationship one to the other. It will be recalled that the patriarchs, individually, had entered into the covenant

[7] Cf. "Forms of Prophetic Literature: the Rhapsody," ch. xviii of R. G. Moulton, *The Literary Study of the Bible* (Boston, 1899).

with God so that they would worship Him alone and that
He would protect them. This personal covenant was broadened in the period of Moses, as a consequence of the Exodus
from Egypt, so that the entire population of Israel became
God's chosen people to recognize and serve Him as the only
God in the world. This covenant, it should be noted carefully, was voluntary on both sides. God elected Israel in
His love and grace, and Israel freely undertook to carry out
the will of God.

According to the prophets, God agreed, for His part,
to reward His faithful people in the land of Israel with
economic prosperity, good health, and peace from all enemies (Deuteronomy 7:12 ff.; and elsewhere). When Israel
prospered, therefore, it could be assumed that her people
had found favor in the sight of the Lord, and prophetic
activity was consequently at a minimum. When, however,
a difficulty arose or threatened to appear, it was a sure sign
that Israel had transgressed against the Covenant and that
God was punishing His people. It was in such times of
crisis and distress that the prophets undertook to determine and expound the reasons for God's anger and the ways
by which the Covenant could be restored.

Since it was not possible for God Himself to transgress
the Covenant, the prophets necessarily sought the causes
of conflict in the actions of the people. If the leaders or the
common folk had worshiped other gods, as in the case of
King Manasseh (II Kings 21), the prophets denounced
those who practiced or tolerated this abomination. Far more
often, however, Israelites broke the Covenant in their relations one with another, and it was such lapses that most frequently provoked the prophets' wrath.

The first obligation laid on the Israelites by the Cove-

nant and the law was the worship of the Lord with prayer
and sacrifice. The prophets deemed these formal aspects
of worship both necessary and good, but they regarded
them as valueless unless fraught with sincerity which found
expression in daily conduct. Isaiah would not accept lip
service as a substitute for active faith and an upright life.
He warns on behalf of God in the majestic first chapter of
his book: '

Bring no more false offerings. Sacrifice is an abomination to
Me. . . . I cannot endure iniquity along with the solemn assembly. . . . Even when you make many prayers, I will not
hear. . . . Wash yourselves, make yourselves clean; put away
your evil doings from before My eyes. Cease to do evil. Learn
to do good. Seek justice. Relieve the oppressed. Take up the
case for the fatherless. Plead for the widow.

All the prophets, from first to last, demanded with stub-
born insistence that the people bring their practices to conform with their beliefs. The teachings of the Lord, epit-
omized in the Torah, the Law of Moses, did not lead to
salvation unless put into daily use. When Saul disobeyed
God's command to destroy all the flocks and herds of the
Amalekites and instead offered up the choicest animals as a
sacrifice, Samuel is reported to have rebuked him, saying:

Has the Lord as great delight in burnt offerings and sacrifices
    as in obeying the voice of the Lord?
Behold, to obey is better than sacrifice,
    and to hearken than the fat of rams [I Samuel 15:22].

Jeremiah denounced mere lip service and empty ritual
time and time again, and on one occasion proclaimed:

Thus says the Lord of Hosts, the God of Israel: Add your burnt
offerings to your sacrifices, and eat the flesh. For I did not speak

to your fathers nor command them in the day that I brought them out of the land of Egypt concerning burnt offerings and sacrifices. But this thing I commanded them, saying, "Obey My voice, and I will be your God, and you shall be My people, and walk in all the way that I command you, that it may be well with you" [7:21–23].

And Amos, well over a century before Jeremiah, had voiced the same conviction (5:21–24) in his famous exhortation which has been quoted ever since:

> But let justice well up as waters,
> and righteousness as a mighty stream.

Nowhere else but in ancient Israel has there been found such persistent and insistent emphasis on doing, on carrying out, not merely on believing in, the teachings of God's spokesmen. That is why Micah was able to put in so few words the essence of Biblical Judaism when he said:

> It has been shown to you, O man, what is good
> and what the Lord requires of you:
> Only to do justice
> and to love loyally
> and to walk humbly with your God [6:8].

This basic principle, that the law had to be obeyed in spirit together with the letter, was summed up even more succinctly in Deuteronomy 16:20, in the three Hebrew words *Tsedek tsedek tirdof*, "Righteous acts, righteous acts shall you pursue." Salvation by faith alone, or by deeds alone, was an unknown doctrine in the Bible; the letter was inseparable from the spirit, even as the act was inseparable from the faith. The insistence on this point may well have arisen from the fact that, difficult as it is to judge the depth and sincerity of purely religious devotion, the justice of a man's acts to his fellows was immediately and inescapably apparent in the small tribal society within which the people of Israel lived. When a merchant was discovered cheating a customer in weighing or measuring, his act was regarded not merely as a civil offense against a fellow Israelite, but much worse as a breach of the Covenant and an abomination of the Lord (Deuteronomy 25:13–16; Leviticus 19:35–37). This sense of equality, moreover, was so strong that a special warning had to be issued that care should be taken that a person not be favored in court merely because he was poor, any more than one be favored because of his wealth: "In righteousness shall you judge your neighbor" (Leviticus 19:15).

All the prophets considered all the Israelites to be equal before the Covenant and in the sight of God, be he king or priest, master or servant, rich or poor. It was this inherent equality which imposed on everyone the personal and inescapable obligation to hear, understand, and obey the divine law. To the prophets, therefore, every act of injustice on the part of one Israelite to another, or of one group against another, was an act of transgression against the Covenant and necessarily brought on appropriate punishment. The function of the prophets was to discern any such iniquities in whatever form, and to persuade the transgressors to repent of their sins and to return to God. This equality before the Covenant raised all men to the common dignity of participating in the Covenant with God.[8]

---

[8] It is erroneous to assert (cf. W. H. Kilpatrick, *Philosophy of Education* [New York, 1951], pp. 72 ff.) that "the Egyptians . . . enriched the world's moral outlook by first asserting the sacredness of human personality"; it is Biblical Israel to whom credit is due for this fundamental cultural development.

The injunction upon each Israelite to deal righteously
with his fellows thereby became more than the defense of
rights of property or persons; it became a defense of human dignity. Thus, if a man was to be lashed in punishment
for a crime, then the maximum number of stripes was to
be forty, "lest, if he should continue to be struck many
stripes above these, your brother should be degraded in
your presence" (Deuteronomy 25:1–3). And if the law for-
bade the gleaning of the vineyard and commanded that "it
should be for the sojourner, the fatherless and the widow,"
it was expressly pointed out that God did so because He
wanted the Israelites to remember that they too were once
helpless slaves, in Egypt (24:21–22).

It has long been recognized that law played an extremely
important part in the life of Israel, but even so, sufficient
attention has not always been paid to the essential nature
of Israel's laws.[9] They established not only the code of
conduct for all Israelites in dealing one with another—
and especially the relations between members of the ruling
classes and the less powerful—but through this code gave
expression to the obligation for just and righteous behavior inherent in the Covenant. The prophets, more than
any other group, emphasized the fact that the laws expressed
God's will or, as one Psalmist said in praise of God and
His Covenant: "Righteousness and justice are the founda-

[9] Cf. the remarks by E. A. Speiser in *Proceedings of the American
Philosophical Society*, XCV (Dec., 1951), 583 ff., on "The pre-
eminent place of the law—*torah*—in the Old Testament and post-
Biblical Judaism [as] . . . a reflection of the unshakable belief that
law was the framework of civilization." See now also Boaz Cohen,
"Letter and Spirit in Jewish and Roman Law," *Mordecai M. Kaplan
Jubilee Volume*, ed. M. Davis, English Section (New York, 1953),
pp. 109–135.

tion of Your throne, steadfast love and truth go before
You" (Psalm 89:15).

Although the prophets are now usually recognized as
the greatest source of inspiration for doctrines of social
reform, they were nevertheless reformers within, rather
than of, their social system. They supported the existing
order and concentrated all their magnificent indignation
on the need to infuse the observance of ritual and legal
regulations with spiritual integrity and a deep sense of
moral justice. It was this emphasis on the spirit of the law
which at once provoked the prophets to their greatest denunciations and exhortations and at the same time brought
them into conflict with the privileged members of their
society. As has generally been the way of the rich and
powerful, the privileged Israelites frequently succumbed
to the temptation to use the law to their advantage; and
while insisting most vehemently on the literal observance
of ritual and legality, they often failed most significantly to
live up to the highest standards implied in the Covenant.
It was failings of this sort that provided the prophets with
the texts for their most eloquent sermons.

Thus it was not social inequality but social injustice
which they denounced, not the existence of rich and poor
within the same society but the abuse of the poor by their
richer brethren which they decried, not the creation of a
new society but the infusion of the Israel they knew with
a new spirit which they demanded. Their basic social philosophy rested on the conviction that if the people expressed their faith in God by obeying His commandments
in their hearts as well as in their acts, the moral climate
of Israel would be purified and the life of her society would
be sound.

The alternative was clear. Transgression of justice and rejection of God's will were sure to be followed by swift and terrible punishment meted out by God Himself. Innumerable examples of this divine retribution are recorded in the Bible. Indeed, the frequency with which the prophetic warnings of doom were fulfilled revived, later on, the concept that prophets are foretellers, a concept which the rhapsodic prophets had abandoned. They were imputed to have the power to call down upon the hapless sinner the curse of heaven. To the prophets themselves, however, neither attribution was justified. Punishment was ordained by God, and the recognition that it would follow unrighteousness was not a secret to be divined by a seer but rather the inescapable conclusion of the Covenant.

The Fate of the Prophets and Their Teachings

It was the fate of the prophets, however, that even within this limited context their teachings were not put into practice. The majestic simplicity and vigor of their language, together with their unswerving concentration on the basic elements of the Hebrew faith and moral code, made it all but impossible for their exhortations to be ignored. When, however, a prophet's denunciation of wrongdoing too strongly swayed the oppressed—if not the oppressors—the ruling classes frequently were forced to pay lip service to the prophetic message in order to maintain or strengthen their hold on the people. Thus the writings of Amos were accepted, to become part of Holy Writ, and used by the secular and priestly rulers to strengthen the institutions of law and public worship. Similarly, the so-called Reformation of Josiah, which Jeremiah first supported enthusiastically, provided one more occasion for the use of prophetic teachings in the special interests of the monarchy and the priesthood of Jerusalem. Vehemently, as the prophets demanded the substance of justice for the orphan and the widow, for the weak and the oppressed, the laws of the kingdom continued to punish ritual transgression more regularly and more severely than moral injustice. The moral code into which the prophets made such magnificent attempt to breathe the spirit of living justice was one of the noblest and most demanding ever produced by man.

One of the outstanding characteristics of the prophets was the forthrightness and conviction with which they addressed themselves to those Israelites, without the least regard for their rank or power, who flouted or perverted the law. Through this uncompromising vehemence, the prophets continually risked and sometimes suffered abuse and even death at the hands of those they attacked. Indeed, believing that all Israelites were equal before the Covenant and in the sight of the Lord, the prophets could hardly have done otherwise than denounce the iniquities of the strong with the same freedom and vigor as those of the weak, and when they suffered it was for their fierce love of the inexorable justice of their God.

Nathan did not hesitate to denounce David the mighty king for his murderous action against Uriah the Hittite (II Samuel 12). Elijah had to flee for his life because of his vehement denunciations of Ahab and Jezebel. Micaiah was hit on the cheek and thrown into prison (I Kings 22:24-27). Amos the Judean risked limb and life when he audaciously invaded the royal sanctuary at Bethel, and he minced no words in telling the royal house and its supporters what lay in store for them as retribution for their rebellion against the Lord. Because he bitterly denounced the domestic and foreign policy of his government, Jeremiah's life was threatened, he was beaten, he was put in stocks, and he was thrown into a dungeon, so that he was constrained to cry out, "And I was like a docile lamb that is led to the slaughter" (11:19). The Second Isaiah echoed these words when he described himself "as a lamb that is led to the slaughter, and as a sheep that is dumb before her shearers" (53:7). Ezekiel was told by God, "And you, son of man, be not afraid of them, neither be afraid of their words, though briers and thorns be with you and you dwell among scorpions" (Ezekiel 2:6). Uriah the prophet was killed by King Jehoiakim (Jeremiah 26:20–23), and the prophet Zechariah was stoned to death (II Chronicles 24:20–21).[10]

Read in a later time and under wholly altered circumstances, the great denunciations appeared to carry meanings which would have been alien, if not repugnant, to the prophets themselves. The announcements of impending doom, which seldom waited long for fulfilment, suggested to later generations the power of foretelling not only swift retribution but, after that, the precise manner of divine intercession for the ultimate restoration of God's people in the land of Israel. Similarly, the sufferings were read as expiatory sacrifices meekly accepted by the prophets to atone for the iniquities of their people, and finally the prophetic insistence on the equality of all before the Cove-

[10] The frequently tragic fate of the prophets became a subject of considerable interest in post-Biblical times, when martyrdom became a recognized concept. Numerous legends grew up about the fate of the prophets, some of which may be found in a little work now known as *The Lives of the Prophets*, recently published in a useful edition by C. C. Torrey (*Journal of Biblical Literature*, Monograph series, I, [Philadelphia, 1946]).

nant was interpreted as belief in a universality encompassing not merely the children of Israel but all men of all nations.

In the great prophecies of doom one of the most common and impressive themes is the warning to the Israelites that unless they hearkened to the word of the Lord they would suffer defeat and even conquest at the hands of their enemies. Thus in the reigns of Jehoiakim, Jehoiachin, and Zedekiah (about 608–586 B.C.), a powerful section of the Judean ruling class wanted to make a pact with Egypt and other countries against Babylonia. Jeremiah, however, openly and uncompromisingly condemned this move as contrary to the will of God and therefore a step toward certain disaster. Instead, he urged a policy of continued cooperation with Babylonia (Jeremiah 25–29; etc.). "Yet you have not listened to Me," Jeremiah said in the name of the Lord, "that you might provoke Me to anger with the work of your hands to your own harm. . . . This whole land shall become a ruin and a waste" (Jeremiah 25:7 ff.).

The same pattern is evident over a century earlier, about 735 B.C., when Isaiah analyzed the efforts of King Pekah of Israel and King Rezin of Aram to force Judah into a coalition against the expanding Assyrian empire (Isaiah 7–8). The prophet advised Judah's government to avoid any such alliance, warning that Israel and her Aramean ally would surely fall. "Behold," he said, "a young woman is with child and shall bear a son, and shall call his name Immanuel. . . . And before the child knows how to refuse the evil and choose the good, the land before whose two kings you are in dread will be deserted" (7:14 ff.).

The historical context makes it clear that the prophets

were, in fact, analyzing with extraordinary acumen the balance of forces in the world of the Levant, and urging their conclusions upon their fellow Israelites with the majestic eloquence of their tradition.[11] Read in this light, the reference to the young woman and her child becomes nothing more than a dramatic measure of time, a warning that before the unborn child will be old enough to know the difference between good and evil, the Lord will bring devastation on Judah's enemies.[12] A similar statement was made by Isaiah in this very connection about his own wife and child, whom he called symbolically Maher-shalal-hash-baz, literally "the spoil speeds, the prey hastes," the double name referring to the two kingdoms of Aram and Israel (Isaiah 8:1–4). Yet when passages of this sort were read in a later and wholly different set of conditions they laid the basis for the common belief that the prophets were foretellers and that their gift was based not merely on their power of analysis of an immediate situation, but that it derived rather from divine inspiration and implied distant and mystical promises.

After the destruction of the Jewish state in 70 A.D., the post-Biblical Jews accepted this concept of prediction as the most significant aspect of prophetic literature. The scrupulous analysis of long-past political and military situa-

[11] Moulton, *op. cit.*, p. 404, put it this way: "Prophecy, in one of its aspects, may be described as the philosophy of history erected into drama." As one case in point among very many, see A. Malamat, "The Historical Setting of Two Biblical Prophecies" [Zechariah 9:1–6 and Jeremiah 47], *Israel Exploration Journal*, I (1950–1951), 149–159.

[12] There has been introduced an additional error, namely, that the pregnant young woman in question was a virgin. The Hebrew word in Isaiah 7:14, *almah*, means "young woman" (even one recently married), not "virgin."

tions no longer concerned the heirs of the Biblical tradition. The literary power of the prophets was such that their works were still read and increasingly searched for meanings relevant to a new age and a new situation. Warnings of defeat and destruction were no longer meaningful after the Dispersion, and the temptation to find hidden promises of restoration and final triumph was overpowering.

Not only did the Jews of the first and second century A.D. read in the prophets a prediction of the new exile and a second restoration, but the early Christians found in the same source predictions of the coming of Jesus and his messianic role. But just as the dubious quality of prediction was only retroactively associated with the prophetic writings, so too was the concept of messianism improperly projected back into the prophetic writings.

It is true that the prophets believed that God would restore His people Israel to their country under the rule of a descendant of the house of David. Anyone who was chosen by the Lord through His prophets to be ruler of His people was regarded as "His messiah," literally, "His anointed." Thus Saul was the "Lord's anointed" (I Samuel 24:7; and frequently), and so were David and Zedekiah (II Samuel 19:22; Lamentations 4:20). Even King Cyrus of Persia, whom the Second Isaiah recognized as God's agent to destroy Babylonia and restore Israel, is described as "His anointed" (Isaiah 45:1). In every case throughout the Biblical period, the "anointed" person was a human being. And when the physical restoration of Israel was contemplated, it was a scion of David who was to be the ruler, the anointed of the Lord. Thus it was Zerubbabel, of the house of David, who led the Restoration of Judah after the Babylonian Exile.

The idea of a superhuman anointed leader, indeed, the very use of the term "Messiah" (with capital "M"), who would be sent down by God at some distant time to intervene directly in behalf of Israel against her oppressors, or in behalf of the righteous against the wicked, is a post-Biblical development in Jewish and Christian circles. Painfully aware that they were unable to cope with the might of Roman imperialism and casting about desperately for comfort and hope in this period of distress and despair, many Jews read back into the Biblical Books the idea and prediction of a superhuman Messiah who would bring deliverance to the Jews at the behest of God. To the Christians, this Messiah was the Christ, which in Greek means "the anointed."

Those who found in the great prophecies the promise of a Messiah tended also to find in the lives of the prophets, with their frequent sufferings, an anticipation of a later, primarily Christian, doctrine of atonement. It became widely assumed that the Second Isaiah, for example, accepted his undeserved suffering meekly and thereby succeeded in sparing his fellow Jews the punishment and doom which was their due for their transgressions against the law and the word of God. According to this doctrine the innocent prophets suffered for the iniquities committed by the people as a whole and served as a substitute for them. There is, however, no basis in the Bible for this principle. It is true that the wickedness of the people was followed by the appearance of the prophets, who as a consequence sometimes suffered abuse; but there is not to be found a single instance in the entire Hebrew Bible where the suffering of a prophet atoned for the sins of a group. Nothing could have been farther from the spirit of the prophetic teachings; that the just and faithful should suffer vicariously, that is, as a substitute, for the unjust and blasphemous, would have been the greatest injustice of all. The prophets insisted on breathing human warmth and understanding into the law, but they never preached a doctrine which superseded the Covenant and which allowed the sacrifice—in any form—of the innocent in place of the guilty.

By the same canon of justice the prophets frequently found that Israel had suffered sufficient punishment for its sins. Repeated statements to this effect can be found in the Bible; the Second Isaiah himself, for example, far from harboring any notions of vicarious atonement, began his series of unsurpassed compositions to his fellow exiles with this tender consolation:

> Comfort ye, comfort ye My people,
>   says your God,
> Speak tenderly to Jerusalem
>   and proclaim unto her
> That her hard service is completed,
>   that her punishment is accepted,
> That she has received of the hand of the Lord
>   double for all her sins [40:1-2].

This concept of vicarious suffering and atonement, then, derives from and has meaning in post-Biblical times when the Jewish state was destroyed and many Jews exiled from the land by the Roman conqueror. It was then, in the rabbinic interpretation, that the "servant of the Lord" in Isaiah 52:13-53:12—who is none other than the prophet himself—came to be identified with the people Israel and Israel came to be regarded as God's servant in suffering vicariously for the sins of the world. Christianity, on the other hand, identified the "servant of the Lord" with Je-

sus. Consequently, the Second Isaiah came to be regarded
as the "suffering" servant of the Lord. In reality, he was
no more a "suffering" servant than Elijah, or Jeremiah, or
Uriah, or Ezekiel. The common term "suffering servant"
is wholly unjustified and misleading in this context.[13]

Particularism and Universality in the Teachings of the Prophets

Another, and perhaps the most important of the concepts anachronistically read back into the tradition of the
prophets was the idea that their teachings broadened out
until they encompassed all humanity in a common brotherhood. One of the most frequently quoted, and erroneously
interpreted, Bible texts is the well-known passage from
Malachi: "Have we not all one father? Has not one God
created us?" (2:10). But this verse has been wrenched
violently out of its original context when it is made to
refer to all mankind. Actually, it charges that the Judean
priests of God "have corrupted the Covenant" of the Lord
(verses 1–9), that all Israel "has profaned the holiness of
the Lord" (verse 11), and that the Lord will punish the
transgressors. Malachi's meaning is no different at this point
than in the first chapter of his Book, where he proposes
that the Lord will destroy Edom if they try to rebuild their
land.[14]

[13] For a useful survey of some of the problems involved, see C. R.
North, *The Suffering Servant in Deutero-Isaiah* (London, 1948);
Rowley, *op. cit.*, chs. i and ii; *Submission in Suffering and Other
Essays on Eastern Thought* (Cardiff, 1951), ch. i.

[14] Of the very few scholars who have noted the essential national-
ism of the Second Isaiah, reference may be made to F. James, *Personalities of the Old Testament* (New York, 1939), p. 263; N. H.
Snaith, in his chapter on "The Servant of the Lord in Deutero-

The prophetic tradition rests squarely on the idea of the Covenant between the Lord and His people Israel. The prophets were concerned directly and exclusively with this "chosen people," and they took notice of other peoples and nations only when the latter came into contact—invariably for bad rather than good—with Judah and Israel. "Hear this word that the Lord has spoken concerning you," Amos said. "You only, have I recognized of all the families of the earth" (3:1–2). The concept of equality between nations would have been incomprehensible to the prophets or their people. It was an idea which could develop only later and under wholly different circumstances and which, not surprisingly, was read back into the prophetic texts by both Jews and Christians when Rome forced the Jews into exile after A.D. 70 and they found themselves adrift in the vast reaches of the Empire.

The land of Israel which the prophets had known was geographically situated at the military crossroads of the ancient Near East. Its population was small and its possibilities of defense slight, with the result that it knew but few extended periods of peace or freedom from fear of Assyria, Aram, Egypt, and Babylonia. The greatest need and desire of Israel was for peace from her neighbors. Her people were not concerned with the international politics or the welfare of Egypt, Moab, Tyre, or Sidon. Their one concern was to be left alone, and it was this overwhelming desire that Isaiah (2:4) and Micah (4:3) expressed in the famous lines:

Isaiah," in *Studies in Old Testament Prophecy*, p. 191; the worthwhile chapter on "The Origin of Hebrew Prophecy" in T. J. Meek, *op. cit.* On Malachi's "thought of the brotherhood of all Israelites, under one Father," see S. R. Driver, *Introduction to the Literature of the Old Testament* (New York, 1914), pp. 355–358.

And [the Lord] shall judge between the nations,
   and He shall decide for many peoples;
And they shall beat their swords into ploughshares,
   and their spears into pruning-hooks.
Nation shall not lift up sword against nation,
   neither shall they learn war any more.[15]

Read wishfully, this majestic passage might be construed, as it so often has, to imply a desire for the brotherhood of men and the universal peace on earth. In hard fact, the context excludes this sentimental interpretation. Isaiah and Micah rigidly predicate any such peace on the triumph of Israel. "Out of Zion shall go forth the law," they say, "and the word of the Lord from Jerusalem."

The Second Isaiah, whose moral outlook is generally regarded as the least exclusivist, consistently proclaimed his strongly national point of view. He assures his fellow exiles:

Thus says the Lord God:
Behold I will lift up My hand to the nations,
   and raise My ensign to the peoples;
And they shall bring your sons in their bosom,
   and your daughters shall be carried upon their shoulders,
And kings shall be your foster-fathers
   and their queens your nursing mothers.
With their face to the earth they shall bow down to you
   and lick the dust of your feet.
And you shall know that I am the Lord [49:22–23].

In a germinal sense, in the sense that he was elementally responsive to the moods and emotions and sufferings of Israel, the Second Isaiah, as the other prophets, came to express

---

[15] The prophet Joel (4:9 ff.; 3:9 ff. in the English versions), in keeping with the prophetic tradition, put this passage to equally nationalistic use.

many ideas that took on great meaning for later generations of Jews and Christians alike. Yet within his own historical setting these ideas applied only to his own people. "Awake, awake," he says:

> Put on your strength, O Zion,
> Put on your glorious garments,
>   Jerusalem, Holy City!
> For there shall no more enter you
>   the uncircumsized and the unclean [52:1].

So speaks the prophet that his own people knew and understood, as they had known and understood Amos, Jeremiah, and the rest before him.

At the same time it would be misleading to leave the impression that the prophets' interest stopped short with their own people Israel and went no further. Israel, dwelling among other nations, was intimately and constantly affected by their actions, and the prophets' attention was repeatedly called to include them. The position of their tiny nation in the midst of other, more powerful, nations led the prophets to an outlook that was universal in its ultimate implications. Believing firmly that their God, the only God in existence, would ultimately deliver them from all threats from other nations, so that no more wars would come upon them, consciously aware that the Torah, their religion, was the only code of laws and life by which man could live, the prophets expressed the conviction that all the peoples of the universe, after they had been through stress and strain at the hands of each other through the will of God, would come to realize that Israel and her religion and her God and His abode on Zion—that these constituted the only proper way of life in the entire world. The gentile peoples of the world would

then come streaming to the mountain of the Lord's house, to
the house of the God of Jacob, in order that, in the words of
Isaiah (2:3) and Micah (4:2):

> He may teach us of His ways
> and we may walk in His paths.
> For out of Zion shall go forth the law,
> and the word of the Lord from Jerusalem.

While it was the civilization of Israel which the prophets
would advocate for the other nations, and while nothing of
the gentile cultures was considered worthy of incorporation
into the Israelite way of life, the particularism of Israel and
her prophetic spokesmen did lay the foundation for the later
concept of universality. Gradually it came to be believed
that all mankind, by adopting unto itself the principles of
Israelite belief and practice—that is by accepting the obligations of the Covenant—might enjoy the fruits of God's
bounty in the manner the God promised His own people
Israel through His prophets. In this universalism, Biblical
Israel and her prophets were unique in the Ancient Near
East.

When the Jewish descendants of the prophets, during the
Hellenistic and especially the Roman periods, became more
fully aware of living in a single great unified society that
encompassed all of the known world, they drew upon and
expanded the universalism of the prophets. The prophetic
concept of the Covenant had aimed at making all men—of
the Israelite society, to be sure—equal in their essential human dignity. This concept, in turn, led to one much broader
in scope, of the universality and inevitability of individual
moral responsibility toward all men, not merely neighbors
and fellow Israelites. It is recorded (Babylonian Talmud,

Shabbat 31a) that during the first century B.C. a heathen approached Hillel, the great exponent of liberalizing Pharisaism in the days of Herod the Great, and asked him for a brief exposition of Judaism. Hillel is said to have replied, "What is hateful to you, do not do to your fellow man. This is the whole Law. The rest is mere commentary." Hillel recognized correctly the implication of the Biblical verse: "And you shall love your neighbor as yourself; I am the Lord" (Leviticus 19:18). This precept was incorporated in Christianity and in the western tradition and transmitted from age to age with tremendous impact.

It is to the prophetic tradition more than any other source that western civilization owes its noblest concept of the moral and social obligations of the individual human being. Even if the prophets preached only to their fellow Israelites and saw justice only in the terms of their Covenant with their God, their ringing words have carried from age to age their belief that justice was for the weak as well as for the strong, that its fulfilment was as much a matter of the spirit as the letter of the law, that one could not serve God at the same time that he mistreated his fellow men, that to love God was to love justice, and that the love of justice placed within the conscience of each human being the ultimate inescapable obligation to denounce evil wherever he saw it, to defy a ruler who commanded him to break the Covenant, and to live in the law and the love of God no matter what the cost.

Chronological Summary ~~~~~~~~~

ALL dates are approximate, and B.C. Of the numerous reasonable reconstructions made of the chronology of the Divided Kingdom, the two most recent, by W. F. Albright in *Bulletin of the American Schools of Oriental Research*, 100 (Dec., 1945), 16–22, and by E. R. Thiele, *The Mysterious Numbers of the Hebrew Kings* (Chicago, 1951), have been employed here, in parallel columns; the reader will not fail to notice that the two systems are usually only a few years apart.

Before 100,000. *Palaeanthropus palestinensis*, chiefly in the Mount Carmel region of Palestine; a mixed race which stood much closer to Cro-Magnon man (*Homo sapiens*) than to the Neanderthal race.

8000–6000. The Natufian or Mesolithic (Middle Stone) Age in Palestine. Grain was cultivated and prepared, but Natufian man was still far more of a food gatherer (hunting, fishing) than a food producer. Domestication of the dog.

6000–4500. The Neolithic (New, or Late, Stone) Age in Palestine. Villages were established, sometimes around shrines. Pottery was introduced. Semites from vast Syrian and

Arabian deserts overran the "Fertile Crescent," sometimes to remain. Increased domestication of animals, e.g., sheep. The Near Eastern Neolithic culture preceded the European by several millennia and influenced it considerably.

4500–3000. The Chalcolithic Age. Copper employed as well as flint. Pottery increasingly common. Writing invented in Mesopotamia. The Jordan and Esdraelon valleys in Palestine settled, as well as other parts of the Near East.

3000–2000. The Early Bronze Age. Emergence of central states in Mesopotamia and Egypt. Semites and Sumerians in control of Mesopotamia. First empire in history, under Sargon of Akkad.

2000–1500. The Middle Bronze Age. Emergence of great empires in western Asia and Egypt. Ascendancy of Amorites (western Semites) and Canaanites in western Asia. The patriarchal period. Babylonian empire of Hammurabi (1726–1686), reduced by Hittites (1550). Palestine under Egyptian control. Hyksos invasion and domination of Egypt (1720–1550) and beginning of Hebrew descent into Egypt.

1500–1200. The Late Bronze Age. Hurrian domination of northern Mesopotamia (the Mitanni Kingdom) (1500–1370), followed by Hittite domination, and then Assyrian (1250). Zenith of Egyptian imperialism ("When Egypt Ruled the East") (1500–1100). Habiru invade and settle in Palestine. Hebrew Exodus from Egypt, under Moses (perhaps shortly after 1300). Wandering in wilderness of Sinai. Conquest of Canaan by Hebrews and Israelites. Term "Israel" first used in triumphal account of campaigns by Merneptah of Egypt (1230).

1200–1000. The Early Iron Age. Egypt in decline. Assyria the main power in Mesopotamia. Collapse of Canaanite power in Palestine. Invasion of Mediterranean coast of Palestine and Syria by the Philistines and other "sea peoples" from the Aegean regions. Habiru on both sides of the Jordan develop into separate nations: Moabites, Ammonites, Edomites, Israelites. Period of the Judges. Hebrew and Israelite tribes in struggle against the Canaanites and others in their midst and round about them. The Philistine threat spurs on most of the tribes to unite under Saul (1020–1005), Israel's first king.

1005–925. The United Israelite Kingdom under David (1005–965) and Solomon (965–925). The Israelite empire was the dominant power in western Asia.

925. The Divided Kingdoms of Israel and Judah.

THE KINGDOM OF JUDAH   THE KINGDOM OF ISRAEL

Horizontal lines indicate a change of dynasty. Overlapping reigns and co-regencies have not been indicated. Where Thiele has offered alternate dates, only the lower of the two has been given here, e.g., 930–909 for his 931/30–910/9 as the dates of Jeroboam I. All the dates are approximate.

KING	REIGN Albright	Thiele	PROPHETS	KING	REIGN Albright	Thiele
Rehoboam	922–915	930–913		Jeroboam I	922–901	930–909
Abijah (Abijam)	915–913	913–910				
Asa	913–873	910–869		Nadab	901–900	909–908
				Baasha	900–877	908–885
				Elah	877–876	885–884
				Zimri (7 days)	876	884
				Tibni		884–880
			E	Omri	876–869	880–873
			L			
Jehoshaphat	873–849	869–848	I	{ Ahab	869–850	873–853
J(eh)oram	849–842	848–841	J	{ Ahaziah	850–849	853–852
			A			
			H			
Ahaziah	842	841	E	{ J(eh)oram	849–842	852–841
Athaliah (usurper)	842–837	841–835	L I	{ Jehu	842–815	841–813
J(eh)oash	837–800	835–796	S H	{ Jehoahaz	815–801	813–798
Amaziah	800–783	796–767	A	{ J(eh)oash	801–786	798–781
Uzziah (Azariah)	783–742	767–739	A M O S	{ Jeroboam II	786–746	781–753
			H O S E A	Zechariah (6 months)	746–745	753–752
			I S A	Shallum (1 month)	745	752
Jotham	742–735	739–732	I A H	Menahem	745–738	752–741
			M	Pekahiah	738–737	741–739
Jehoahaz I (Ahaz)	735–715	731–715	I C	Pekah	737–732	739–731
			A H	Hoshea	732–724	731–722
				Fall of Samaria to Assyria	722/1	723/2
Hezekiah	715–687	715–686				
Invasion of Judah by Sennacherib of Assyria, 701						
Manasseh	687–642	686–641				

THE KINGDOM OF JUDAH

KING	REIGN		PROPHETS
	Albright	*Thiele*	

KING	Albright	Thiele	PROPHETS
Amon	642–640	641–639	
Josiah	640–609	639–608	
Jehoahaz II (Shallum) (3 months)	609	608	
Jehoiakim (Eliakim)	609–598	608–597	J E R E M I A H
Jehoiachin (Jeconiah) (3 months)	598	597	
First phase of Babylonian Exile 598/597			
Zedekiah (Mattaniah)	598–587	597–586	
Fall of Jerusalem to Babylonia	587	586	

Second (and major) phase of Babylonian Exile 587/586
Governor Gedaliah assassinated, 582
Third phase of Babylonian Exile 582

592–570	Ezekiel the prophet in Babylonia.
550–540	The Second Isaiah, prophet in Babylonia.
539	First Return to Judah; Edict of Liberation by Cyrus of Persia.
515	Zerubbabel and Joshua, secular and religious heads of Judea. Haggai and Zechariah, prophets in Judea. Temple in Jerusalem rebuilt.
400	Second return to Judah, under Ezra. Jewish colonies in Egypt. Jewish theocracy established in Judea by Ezra and Nehemiah. The high priests rule Judea.
300	Hellenistic civilization overwhelms Western Asia and Egypt, following on the conquests by Alexander the Great.

Suggestions for Further Reading~

IN understanding the development of western civilization the Bible is unquestionably the most important single text, and no heir to this tradition who has not read it can consider himself educated. Of the translations available in English the best are *The Revised Standard Version of the Old Testament* (New York, 1952), *The Old Testament—an American Translation,* rev. ed. by T. J. Meek (Chicago; several printings), and *The Holy Scriptures according to the Masoretic Text,* editor-in-chief M. L. Margolis (Jewish Publication Society, Philadelphia, 1917). In spite of the tremendous contribution of the King James version not only to literary style but to the formation of the character within the English-speaking tradition, this translation is unfortunately not sufficiently accurate to be useful in connection with Hebraic history. For those who would consult an introduction along critical lines there is G. B. Gray, *A Critical Introduction to the Old Testament* (London, 1919); a more conservative approach is followed in S. B. Freehof's *Preface to Scripture* (Cincinnati, 1950). Only in more recent times has the Hebrew Bible been treated as literature. Richard G. Moulton, *The Literary Study of the Bible,* rev. ed. (Boston, 1899), and the companion volume, *The Modern Reader's Bible* (New York, 1930), are worth reading. Any of J. A. Bewer, *The Literature of the Old Testament,* rev. ed. (New York, 1933), Mary E. Chase, *The Bible for the Common Reader* (New York,

1945), and A. Lods, *Histoire de la littérature Hébraïque et Juive*, etc. (Paris, 1950), will be rewarding to the reader—though they all require revision in the evaluation of the historical background. A brief evaluation of "Hebrew Literature," including the Biblical, may be found in E. Silberschlag's chapter (pp. 175–212) in *The World through Literature* (New York, 1951). The Biblical literature is treated in broad perspective by H. M. and N. K. Chadwick, *The Growth of Literature* (2 vols., Cambridge, 1936), in Vol. II, pp. 629–777. The specifically Near Eastern background may be gauged in T. H. Gaster's retelling of some of *The Oldest Stories in the World* (New York, 1952).

The history of the Biblical period is subject to more frequent and serious change than any other, both because of the constant discovery of new texts and materials and the consequent reinterpretation of the older data. Whoever wishes to keep up with the latest discoveries and trends in the history of ancient Israel would do well to read regularly *The Biblical Archaeologist*, ed. G. E. Wright (American Schools of Oriental Research, New Haven, subscription $1.00 per year, for four issues). Ralph E. Turner's *The Great Cultural Traditions, the Foundations of Civilization* (2 vols., New York and London, 1941), serves as a useful introduction to the ancient world in general, though the specific sections on ancient Israel (pp. 329–359, 697–734) need revision. Useful books on the beginnings of history are V. Gordon Childe's *Man Makes Himself* (Mentor Books, 1951) and *New Light on the Most Ancient East*, 4th ed. (London, 1952). A serviceable popular survey of the ancient Near East is S. Moscati, *Geschichte und Kultur der semitischen Völker* (Stuttgart, 1953). *Ancient Near Eastern Texts relating to the Old Testament*, ed. J. B. Pritchard (Princeton, 1950; the companion volume, *The Ancient Near East in Pictures*, will appear in 1954), is an excellent collection of documents which shed direct and indirect light on the Hebrew Bible. *The Intellectual Adventure of Ancient Man*, ed. H. and H. A. Frankfort (Chicago, 1946), with chapters on Egypt (by J. A. Wilson), Mesopotamia (by T. Jacobsen), and the Hebrews (by W. A. Irwin), is an integrated attempt to explain the thinking of the ancient Near East.

The historical geography of Palestine has been very well treated by G. E. Wright and F. V. Filson in *The Westminster Historical Atlas to the Bible* (Philadelphia, 1945); the text of this book constitutes also a fine sketch of Biblical Israel's history. The same may be said of N. Glueck, *The River Jordan, being an Illustrated Account of Earth's Most Storied River* (Philadelphia, 1946). An up-to-date history of ancient Israel is not available as yet. A well-ordered and stimulating attempt to reconstruct the origin and development of Israel, her Law, her concept of God, her priesthood and prophets, may be found in T. J. Meek's *Hebrew Origins*, rev. ed. (New York, 1950). A compact sketch of "The Biblical Period," by W. F. Albright, constitutes Chap. I in *The Jews*, ed. L. Finkelstein (Philadelphia, 5710–1949); with which may be read profitably the same author's chapter on "The Old Testament World," in *The Interpreter's Bible*, Vol. I (New York–Nashville, 1952), pp. 233–271. Cyrus H. Gordon's *Introduction to Old Testament Times* (Ventnor, N.J., 1953) and F. James' *Personalities of the Old Testament* (New York, 1945) are the best of their kind.

Selected Bibliography for Teachers and Advanced Readers

In addition to *The Biblical Archaeologist*, the more advanced student should consult the *Bulletin of the American Schools of Oriental Research*, ed. W. F. Albright. The annual *Book List* published by the British Society for Old Testament Research (ed. H. H. Rowley, Manchester University, England) and the virtually exhaustive bibliographic listing of books and articles in the Biblical and related fields in the journal *Biblica* are also useful tools for keeping abreast of the latest literature and developments.

When the revised *Cambridge Ancient History* appears, there will be available an up-to-date history of the entire ancient Near East; E. Meyer's *Geschichte des Altertums* and H. R. H. Hall's *Ancient History of the Near East* likewise need very considerable revision. A. Scharff–A. Moortgat, *Ägypten und Vorderasien im Altertum* (München, 1950) is the best available. In *Forgotten Religions*, ed. V. Ferm (New York, 1950), may be found very good chapters on the religion of the Sumerians, Assyrian-Babylonians, Canaanites, and Hittites. A. J. Toynbee's *Study of History* (London, 1947) has rightly been rejected by specialists as having very little validity for the ancient Near East. J. Finegan's *Light from the Ancient Past* (Princeton, 1946) is a reliable survey, archaeologically slanted, of the Fertile Crescent in antiquity; his companion volume, *The Archeology of World Religions* (Princeton, 1952), deals with Zoroastrianism, Islam, and the Far East. S. N. Kramer's *Sumerian Mythology* (Philadelphia, 1944) and his subsequent articles in such publications as *Journal of the American Oriental Society* and *Journal of Cuneiform Studies* (cf. his fascinating account of "A 'Fulbright' in Turkey," *University [of Pennsylvania] Museum Bulletin*, Dec., 1952); C. H. Gordon's *Ugaritic Literature* (Rome, 1949); T. H. Gaster's *Thespis: Ritual, Myth and Drama in the Ancient Near East* (New York, 1950)—all provide a useful background for the Biblical literature. A. Heidel has written two works worth consulting, *The Babylonian Genesis, the Story of Creation*, rev. ed. (Chicago, 1951), and *The Gilgamesh Epic and Old Testament Parallels*, rev. ed. (Chicago, 1953). J. A. Wilson's *The Burden of Egypt* (Chicago, 1951) is a significant interpretation of ancient Egyptian culture. O. R. Gurney's *The Hittites* (Pelican Books, 1952) is already the standard work on the subject. For a brief evaluation of the ancient Near East as an abiding and contributing factor to the problems of the Near East of our own times, see Pt. I, "The Background," of E. A. Speiser, *The United States and the Near East* (Cambridge, 1947).

The standard work on the historical geography of Palestine is F. M. Abel's *Géographie de la Palestine* (2 vols., Paris, 1933–1938). A. J. Brawer's *Land of Israel* (in Hebrew; Tel Aviv, 5711–1951) is more broadly conceived. Two useful works are B. Maisler, *The Graphic Historical Atlas of Palestine, 2000–333* B.C. (English and Hebrew editions; Tel Aviv and Jerusalem, 1941), and H. G. May–C. C. McCown–J. S. Kates, *The Remapping of the Bible World, Nelson's New Bible Maps* (New York, 1949). M. Burrows' *What Mean These Stones?* (New Haven, 1941), C. C. McCown, *The Ladder of Progress in Palestine* (New York, 1943), and W. F. Albright, *The Archaeology of Palestine* (Pelican Books, 1949), constitute authoritative introductions to Biblical archaeology. E. L. Sukenik's chapter on the "History of Jewish Archaeology" in *The Jewish People, Past and Present*, Vol. I (New York, 1946), pp. 48–77, is the best available. C. H. Gordon's *The Living Past* (New York, 1941) is an interestingly written introduction to the rediscovery of the ancient Near East. E. Chiera's *They Wrote on Clay* (Chicago, 1938) is useful in this connection.

An up-to-date detailed history of ancient Israel is not available as yet. T. H. Robinson–W. O. E. Oesterley, *A History of Israel* (Oxford, 1932), has many good features, though it did not utilize adequately the archaeological materials available at the time. The same may be said of the two volumes by A. Lods, *Israel from its Beginnings to the Middle of the Eighth Century* (New York, 1932) and *The Prophets and the Rise of Judaism* (New York, 1937). W. F. Albright's two works, *From the Stone Age to Christianity, Monotheism and the Historical Process* (Baltimore, 1940) and *Archaeology and the Religion of Israel* (Baltimore, 1942), although somewhat difficult, will prove rewarding reading to every student who wishes to probe into the character of Israel's history and religion. Albrecht Alt and Martin Noth have added notably to our knowledge of the Biblical world; the former's monographs, *Der Gott der Väter* (Stuttgart,

1929) and *Die Ursprünge des israelitischen Rechts* (Leipzig, 1934), are now being issued, together with several other studies, in 2 volumes as *Kleine Schriften zur Geschichte des Volkes Israel* (1953); and the latter's *Das System der Zwölf Stämme Israels* (Stuttgart, 1930), *Überlieferungsgeschichtliche Studien* (2 vols., Halle, 1943, 1948), *Geschichte Israels* (Göttingen, 1950), and *Die Welt des Alten Testaments*, 2nd ed. (Berlin, 1953), among many others, are good examples of their fine scholarship. A number of E. Dhorme's important articles have been brought together to form *Receuil Édouard Dhorme, Études bibliques et orientales* (Paris, 1951). R. de Vaux's writings are always worth reading, such as his series of articles on "Les Patriarches hébreux et les découvertes modernes" in *Revue biblique* (since 1946), and his long article on "Israël (Peuple d')" in Supplément IV (1947–1948), columns 729–777 of F. Vigouroux, *Dictionnaire de la Bible*. J. Pedersen's *Israel, its Life and Culture*, pts. I–IV (Copenhagen, 1926 and 1940), and Max Weber's studies of *Ancient Judaism*, trans. and ed. by H. H. Gerth–D. Martindale (Glencoe, Ill., 1952), merit careful study.

The best Biblical encyclopedia is the Hebrew *Encyclopaedia Biblica* (Jerusalem, 1950–); Vol. I covers the first letter of the Hebrew alphabet. The French *Dictionnaire de la Bible*, ed. F. Vigouroux (5 vols., Paris, 1895–1912), with numerous *Suppléments*, ed. L. Pirot and A. Robert, is very good. *The Westminster Dictionary of the Bible*, 5th ed., by H. S. Gehman (Philadelphia, 1944), is the best of the one-volume reference works. See further C. T. Fritsch's discussion of "Bible Dictionaries and Encyclopedias" in *Interpretation*, I (July, 1947), pp. 363–371. A. E. Bailey's book on *Daily Life in Bible Times* (New York, 1943) and M. S. and J. L. Miller's *Encyclopedia of Bible Life* (New York and London, 1944) are useful reference works for matters dealing with the everyday life of ancient Israel. The Israel (formerly, Jewish Palestine) Exploration Society has issued an excellent Hebrew *Library of Palestinology*, ed. by S. Yeivin (nine little volumes appeared since 1936).

Among the more detailed introductions to the Bible, S. R. Driver, *Introduction to the Literature of the Old Testament*, rev. ed. (New York, 1913), Otto Eissfeldt, *Einleitung in das Alte Testament* (Tübingen, 1934), and R. H. Pfeiffer, *Introduction to the Old Testament* (New York and London, 1941), are outstanding. There is no single up-to-date series of commentaries on the different Biblical books; *The Cambridge Bible for Schools and Colleges*, ed. A. F. Kirkpatrick, and *The Soncino Books of the Bible*, ed. A. Cohen, constitute two serviceable series of brief and popular commentaries on each book of the Old Testament; the same may be said of the commentary series by M. H. Segal, *The Law, the Prophets and the Hagiographa, a Literary Edition* (in Hebrew; Tel Aviv, 1947 ff.). The exegetical part of *The Interpreter's Bible* (New York–Nashville, 1952 ff.) will prove useful; of the Old Testament, only Vols. I and II (General and Old Testament articles: Genesis–Samuel, Ruth) have appeared to date.

There are some excellent works on the history of the text and translations of the Hebrew Bible. The best among them are M. L. Margolis' little book on *The Story of Bible Translations* (Philadelphia, 1917), H. B. Swete's exhaustive *Introduction to the Old Testament in Greek*, rev. ed. by R. R. Ottley (Cambridge, 1914), and B. J. Roberts' clear and up-to-date *The Old Testament Text and Versions* (Cardiff, 1951). H. G. May has written an interesting account of *Our English Bible in the Making* (Philadelphia, 1952); two other works useful in this connection are *The Bible in its Ancient and English Versions*, ed. H. Wheeler Robinson (Oxford, 1940), and I. M. Price, *The Ancestry of Our English Bible*, rev. by W. A. Irwin and A. P. Wikgren (New York, 1949).

On the present state of Biblical research, the student may consult *The Study of the Bible Today and Tomorrow* (chapters by twenty-four different scholars), ed. H. R. Willoughby (Chicago, 1947), and *The Old Testament and Modern Study* (contributions by twelve scholars), ed. H. H. Rowley (Oxford, 1951).

There is not yet available a standard work on the theology of the Old Testament; the most ambitious and detailed attempts at writing one are W. Eichrodt's *Theologie des Alten Testaments* (3 vols., 1933–1939) and Yehezkel Kaufman's *History of the Israelite Religion*, etc. (in Hebrew, 7 vols., Tel Aviv, 1937 ff.). The various works on the subject, Christian and Jewish, tend too much to read into the text and thought of the Hebrew Bible the features of Christianity and Judaism which came into being long after the Biblical period terminated. There is likewise the methodologically and historically incorrect approach according to which the history and religion of the Israelites as expressed in the Hebrew Bible constitute but the preparation for the New Testament, Judaism being treated as but the preliminary phase of Christianity. G. E. Wright has rightfully protested against this view in his *Challenge of Israel's Faith* (Chicago, 1944); and see in this connection N. H. Snaith, *The Distinctive Ideas of the Old Testament* (London, 1944). R. B. Y. Scott, *The Relevance of the Prophets* (New York, 1944), is worth reading. O. J. Baab, G. W. Anderson, and N. W. Porteous have contributed convenient surveys of recent studies in Biblical theology, the first-mentioned in *The Study of the Bible Today and Tomorrow* (ed. H. R. Willoughby), pp. 401–418, and the last two in *The Old Testament and Modern Study* (ed. H. H. Rowley), pp. 283–310, 311–345. O. J. Baab has written also a sober account of *The Theology of the Old Testament* (New York, 1949). H. W. Smith's *Man and His Gods* (Boston, 1952) is worth careful reading.

The reader who wishes to pursue the history of the Jews in the period of the Second Jewish Commonwealth, and subsequently, may turn to S. Grayzel's popular *History of the Jews from the Babylonian Exile to the End of World War II* (Philadelphia, 5707–1947). M. L. Margolis–A. Marx, *A History of the Jewish People* (Philadelphia, 1927), is a good reference book. A more up-to-date and detailed reference work is S. W. Baron, *A Social and Religious History of the Jews*, 2d ed., Vols. I and II "Ancient Times" (Philadelphia, 5712–1952), covering the period from the patriarchs to the Talmud; several subsequent volumes will continue the story down to our own times. *The Legacy of Israel* (Oxford, 1927), ed. E. R. Bevan and C. Singer, is easily the best of its kind. M. Lowenthal's unusually fascinating account of *The Jews of Germany, a Story of Sixteen Centuries* (Philadelphia, 1936) gives a very good idea of the career of the Jews in the diaspora. C. F. Moore's three volumes on *Judaism in the First Centuries of the Christian Era* (Harvard, 1927–1930) make thoughtful reading. An authoritative history of the Jews in the Hellenistic and Roman periods (the Second Jewish Commonwealth proper) is being prepared for publication by S. Zeitlin; see in the meantime his *Prolegomena to a History of the Second Jewish Commonwealth* (Philadelphia, 1933), *Who Crucified Jesus?*, 2d ed. (New York, 1947), and numerous articles in the *Jewish Quarterly Review* (especially since 1930). A convenient handbook for this period is R. H. Pfeiffer, *History of New Testament Times, with an Introduction to the Apocrypha* (New York, 1949).

Index

All place names have been localized on at least one of the five maps; thus Jerusalem (II B 4-5) indicates that Jerusalem may be identified in Map II, B longitudinally, and 4-5 latitudinally.